'The Christian vocation to li[ve in]
the city requires a long-term [commitment]
– living and working with th[e people.]
Living patiently, consistentl[y ... so that]
we understand the unique and evolving [needs of]
the people and the call. This book reflects the wisdom gleaned in
decades of such dedication and sincere faith.'
Marijke Hoek, theologian and writer

'Paul Keeble is one of those rare people who have felt called by
God to live in the inner city long term. Many come to areas of
deprivation out of a sense of call, stay for a few years, and then
move on and move out. Not so with Paul. He has stayed and
stayed. This means that we should listen very attentively to what
he says in this new book. Drawing on a wide range of mission
theologians and practitioners who have lived and served in areas
of multiple deprivation, he develops the important concept of
"mission-with" as the model for authentic Christian engagement
with the inner city – and elsewhere. He roots this in the ministry
of Jesus, especially His incarnation and the wider teachings of
Scripture. It is a timely, authentic, powerful and important book
that deserves attention from practitioners, academics and church
leaders alike. I warmly commend it.'
Rt Rev Mark Ashcroft, Bishop of Bolton

'I first got to know Paul Keeble some 16 years ago. But for more
than twice as long as that, Paul and his wife Judith have lived in
inner-city Manchester. They are there, not by accident, but as a
result of a deliberate decision to live truly Christlike lives that, to
use Paul's own phrase, "can be observed" by their neighbours. If
your understanding of mission is conditioned by evangelistic
events or church projects this book will challenge your thinking
and cause you to reassess your priorities.

'The integrity and humility of Paul's life, the credibility
earned by his long years of commitment to the inner city, and the

intellectual rigour of his thinking mean that this is a book which will make you rethink such hackneyed phrases as "incarnational living". I wholeheartedly recommend it.'
Chick Yuill, speaker and writer

'It's the very ordinariness of the narrative that gripped me from the first: the unheroic reality of living faithfully in, among and with people, and so expressing deep love. The ordinary courage and obedience of entering into God's mission of grace for an entire community is demonstrated with subtlety, reflection and care. Paul Keeble's story-telling is deeply thoughtful, and the theology it forms in this book grips your imagination and helps you breathe. You realise that *here is urban mission*, a description, guide, companion and way of thinking that challenges some of the transactional ways the church wants to work. It provokes questions and advocates instead for a present, personal and humble being, serving God in a rooted community. I highly commend this book and its author.'
Rev Dr Deirdre Brower-Latz, Principal, Nazarene Theological College, Manchester

'We make the mistake as Christians of thinking we are taking God with us into any given situation. God is already there; our mission is to find what God is doing and join in. "Mission-with" is a missing element in Christianity today. Paul Keeble outlines a theological approach which is impressively demonstrated in his life, and this book helps us to understand that approach in a very practical way.'
Michael Harvey, Developer of Back to Church Sunday

'Paul Keeble writes about Manchester's inner city, our inner city, with love and care because he has long been part of it. Faith may move mountains, but it is the commitment to community and belief in the people who make up the community/ies of inner urban Manchester that has seen people like Paul invest their lives over many years, driven by the feeling that we should and could do better. There was no naivety in this, no magic solutions, but a real faith and understanding that local people working together could bring about change, and together they did. Those who come to areas beset with the challenges of poverty and the many hardships it inflicts may come only to speak with the seductive tongue of angels, and are but that resounding gong. Those who come to offer love to the people who make up that community can, as part of that community, help change their world, and that for the better.'

Tony Lloyd, Greater Manchester Mayor and Police and Crime Commissioner

'Paul Keeble's book is a timely challenge to us all, lay and ordained alike, to rethink how the church makes its decisions about ministry and mission – and to start doing it Jesus' incarnational way. Paul tells us about the theory, but more importantly, this is learning from the real experience of committed Christian living.'

Bishop Laurie Green, urban theologian, author, Chair of the National Estate Churches Network

'Mission is challenging to us all in one way or another, often to the point where we do little of it, especially in our own communities. That's what makes Paul Keeble's book a most important read. Here is a family who decided to live – and stay – in an inner-city location, rather than move out to somewhere more affluent and comfortable. And they didn't see mission as something to be "done" to people, but rather with and alongside those who live there. Yes, it's challenging, but it's also a very interesting story which I believe will actually be an encouragement to all who read it.'

Rob White, Co-founder of Hope for Justice, author

MISSION-WITH

SOMETHING OUT OF THE ORDINARY

PAUL KEEBLE

instant
apostle

First published in Great Britain in 2017

Instant Apostle
The Barn
1 Watford House Lane
Watford
Herts
WD17 1BJ

British Library Cataloguing-in-Publication Data

A catalogue record for this book is available from the British Library

This book and all other Instant Apostle books are available from Instant Apostle:

Website: www.instantapostle.com

E-mail: info@instantapostle.com

ISBN 978-1-909728-60-8

Printed in Great Britain

Instant Apostle is a pioneering publishing house that exists to inspire followers of Jesus and promote the values of His Kingdom in the world.

Instant Apostle was founded to publish books by writers who are passionate about addressing diverse social issues from a Kingdom perspective – in any and every genre. Whether it is faith-building autobiography, riveting fiction, engaging study in Christian mindfulness or compassionate response to mental health problems, if a book is well written, original and authentic you will find it with us. We want to share Kingdom values with everyone, and publish titles that cross into secular markets, particularly in adults' and children's fiction.

Instant Apostle books engage with varied and poignant subjects, from child sex-trafficking and autism to the plight of asylum seekers and the challenges of young people growing up in the social media age. These are books by informed, creative and sometimes opinionated people that demolish stale paradigms and foster faith in Jesus.

Working with established writers and actively welcoming new authors, Instant Apostle seeks out prophetic voices that will change the way readers young and old understand God's Kingdom and see the world! Are you ready to join us?

Share the passion. Get reading. Get writing. Get published!

Acknowledgements

Thank you to …

Our inner-city natives: Holly, Alannah, Daniel.
Our Brunswick church family.
Neighbours past and present: our friends, partners, helpers and teachers.
Rev Martin and Mrs Carol Gooder.
Marijke Hoek.
Gordon (my reader).
Harbour Street fellowship and all those who pray for and support us.
Derek Purnell and the trustees and associates of Urban Presence.
Friends, family, co-workers and encouragers.

The Gladstone Library, Hawarden, in particular Rev Dr Peter Francis, for support and a great place to concentrate.

The Urban Theology Unit in Sheffield, in particular Rev Dr John Vincent, my MPhil supervisor, and Rev Dr Ian Duffield for creative suggestions as I developed this book from the MPhil thesis.

Most of all, Judith – with me throughout all that follows…

For Daniel

Contents

Foreword

I first got to know Paul and Judith in the second half of the 1980s when I was invited on several occasions to speak at Brunswick Church. Paul was working with a band for Youth for Christ at the time, and we also met up at a couple of events in London during those years. As a couple, as members, they had committed to live in the local area, and were raising a young family. Our sons often played together. I was always impressed with Paul and Judith's commitment to the urban city of Manchester! So easily, after university they could have done what so many Christians did: retreat to suburbia for their comfort and safety. But instead they chose to live an incarnational ministry.

Then in 2002 I went to Manchester to help with the follow-up meetings after the Gangstop march. There was Paul, still living in the area and now one of the local residents affected by gang violence and wanting to take action to respond. We worked together in the formation of that response, a community organisation called Carisma, and later on, with the first Street Pastors project in Manchester, one of the first outside London.

This book tells the story of those years as a living testimony of Paul's life and journey as he seeks to bring the Kingdom of God to the city where he lives. It is not just about his academic theological views but also about how he has practically lived these out over many years.

I have walked the streets of inner-city Manchester with Paul while most others are safely tucked up in their beds. He has been incredibly supportive of his local community, playing a significant role in developing the work of Street Pastors and other strategic initiatives.

His ministry is right at the heart of the city of Manchester and this book speaks not only of God's Kingdom but also of a holistic approach to establishing that Kingdom here right now. Paul is an inspiration to me and others in the churches and across the UK.

Thank you, Paul, for this book.

Rev Les Isaac OBE
CEO Ascension Trust, founder of Street Pastors

Trembling hearts, mingle beatings.
Our great adventure is living to love.
Hurting and praying, life and death weighing.
Shallow and human, touched by divine.
And when you look beneath the surface,
You will find, more to this than meets the eye.

Geoff Mann[1]

---

[1] 'More To This' from the album *Loud Symbols* by A Geoff Mann Band, 1990. Used by kind permission.

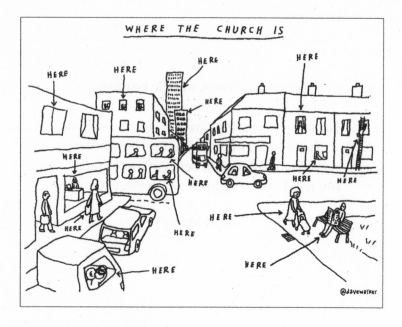

Illustration copyright © Dave Walker. www.cartoonchurch.com
Used with permission.

Introduction

I was standing with my friend Marijke in Platt Fields, a city park in inner-south Manchester. It was dusk on a clear spring day and we were watching a Family Lantern Parade for Peace led by a samba band approaching the park's Peace Garden by the lake. The marchers – a nice snapshot sample of our local multi-ethnic community – had just passed a local BBC News reporter and camera crew doing a live broadcast to the early evening news. With us were Tom O'Callaghan, that year's Mayor of Manchester, and Gerald Kaufman, the local Member of Parliament, who were waiting to unveil several mosaics made by local schoolchildren. Local children had also made the lanterns that were illuminating the marchers and reflecting in the water, and had recorded the peace-themed songs playing on a small sound system behind us. The young people were excited and justifiably proud of their handiwork. Two Muslim girls in particular, when 'their' song came on, were telling anyone who would listen that it was them singing on the speaker.

This was the climax of the 2005 PeaceWeek, eight days of events and activities organised by Carisma, a community group I had worked with others to form as a grass-roots response to the 'guns and gangs' issue that had dominated our area for some years. Marijke turned to me and said, 'This is mission *with* the community.'

That remark began what I later came to call a 'theological back-fill',[1] as it began a process for me of reflecting back on how I, from a middle/upper working-class white suburban background in Northern Ireland, came to be a long-term resident in an ethnically mixed area of inner-city Manchester, and part of a positive community response to gang violence.

That story could be summed up in the words 'where' and 'what'. It is about my relocating to *where* I felt a sense of calling to be – a neighbourhood that few, if any, of my university-educated peers would aspire to live in – and then *what* I did when I got there.

But more than that, how can the word 'mission' be applied to something not led or organised by a church, with no overt proclamation of the gospel, or even leaflets inviting everyone to a Guest Service? My process of reflection was also about the concurrent growth of my theological understanding of Christian mission, as influenced by my experience in this context, and in turn influencing further experience. In other words, certain incidents and actions brought about changes in my thinking, and those changes in my thinking had led to my taking certain further actions, as reflection and practice interact.

I have found the word 'praxis', meaning 'reflective action', a useful term to denote this interaction. Praxis has been more fully defined as 'reflection and action upon the world in order to transform it'.[2] Similar to the 'hermeneutical circle' of Liberation Theology, action is reflected on, brought to the Bible, and this informs further action, and so on. More than that, it is action 'which embodies certain qualities. These include a commitment to human well-being and the search for truth, and respect for others'.[3]

This book is about a theological model of Christian mission, specifically giving validity and a name to a way of practising mission which I believe is going on but largely unrecognised, and which can complement and enrich other expressions of mission. 'Mission-with' has not been thought up in a vacuum or a classroom, but through reflecting on experience and activity in a particular context: a particular area of inner-city Manchester that I and my wife moved to as 'incomers' in 1980. While the book is not intended to be an autobiography, our story is used to illustrate how the model came about and has operated in real-life situations. Its development, together with that of my practice and theology of mission (in that order) runs through the chronology of the story.

Telling the story, first the 'where' and then the 'what', with each followed by some theological reflections, forms parts two and three of the book. Part one sets the scene with a brief pen-picture of our area of Manchester, and some comments on incomers, specifically '*Christian* incomers'. It then describes the 'mission-with' model and the theology of mission behind it. This section jumps the chronology somewhat, and you may wish to refer back to it after reading the story, but I think it is good to have a comprehension of the concepts and see how they evolved as the story unfolds.

Part four looks at 'mission-with' in wider contexts. As the model was born out of a relocation to the inner city, I will examine the broader issue of where Christians live, looking at themes such as incarnation and discipleship. Elements of 'mission-with' can be found in many other models of mission, so I will then survey a number of those models and consider the extent to which they share features in common or contrast with 'mission-with'.

Finally, I draw conclusions, do some evaluating of the model and assess its significance and implications for local churches and Christian mission.

---

[1] A term I came up with at the time to describe a process of reflection *after* action – rather than before or during – asking what was happening here theologically. I subsequently became aware of the parallel to the Liberation Theology concept of theology as the 'second act'.

[2] Paulo Friere, *Pedagogy of the Oppressed* (London: Penguin, 1996) p.33.

[3] M. K. Smith (1999, 2011). 'What is Praxis?' in *the encyclopaedia of informal education*, http://www.infed.org/biblio/b-praxis.htm (accessed 4th October 2016).

Part One

Setting the Scene

Mission and the 'mission-with' model

'Mission-with' is simply 'presence-among' – *being with* people – and 'project-praxis' – *doing with* people. It is dependent on a wide view of mission – seeing it as joining in with God's Mission (the *missio Dei*) to bring *shalom* or wholeness to His creation (more on these concepts below). Mission therefore includes what has been traditionally seen as evangelism, or bringing a message *to* – which I have called 'mission-to' – and social action, doing acts of service *for* – which I have called 'mission-for'. 'Mission-with' is a distinct further category of mission praxis to be set alongside these two, consisting of being a 'presence-among', and the resultant personal praxis, doing the ordinary things of life that everybody does; and 'project-praxis' – action for well-being and the common good arising from being present and having shared concerns with fellow residents.

The 'mission-with' model and with it my theology of mission have slowly emerged during my years as an incomer in inner-city Manchester and through my ordinary life there and the various projects in which I have joined with others. This section goes into the model in more depth, but to lead into it I first need to explain more fully my understanding of what mission is, as this undergirds the 'mission-with', and also describe 'mission-to' and 'mission-for'.

So what, exactly, is mission?

For some, mission is quite easy to define; for others it is a lot harder to pin down neatly (I see that elusiveness in lots of our efforts to describe the things of God). These correspond to narrow and wide views of what mission is. The theologians Keith Ferdinando and David Bosch are advocates of the two approaches. While my view has largely moved from narrow to wide, I maintain that each retains weaknesses and strengths. So, still not cut and dried.

In *Transforming Mission*, David Bosch indicates how difficult it is to define mission and maintains that the early Church made no conscious attempts to do so in any explicit way. New Testament writers such as Matthew, Luke and Paul were 'defining and redefining what the church was called to do in the world of their day'[1] as part of a formulation of theology 'on the hoof'. They 'were not scholars who had the leisure to research the evidence before they put pen to paper. Rather, they wrote in the context of an "emergency situation", of a church which, because of its missionary encounter with the world, was *forced* to theologise'.[2] This echoes Liberation Theology's concept of theology as the 'second act', and also resonates with my 'theological back-fill' reflecting on praxis (eg forming Carisma), at the time undertaken instinctively. Definitions of mission are a far more recent phenomenon, particularly since the upsurge of mission and missions in the nineteenth century,[3] and have consistently struggled to give full expression to something which is 'a multi-faceted ministry in respect of witness, service, justice, healing, reconciliation, liberation, peace, evangelism, fellowship, church planting, contextualisation, and much more'.[4]

Bosch roots mission in the concept of the *missio Dei* – God as a missionary God, constantly looking to deepen relationship with His creation – involving 'God's activity, which embraces both the church and the world, and in which the church may be privileged to participate'.[5] As such it pre-dates, is far more than, and is not limited to the praxis of the Church. So, mission is, in its simplest sense, Christians participating in, and continuing, the work of God as practised by Jesus.[6] Or, as it has often been put: finding out what God is doing and joining in.

In short, mission is what the Church was founded to do. This is why it is here. As I heard it put many years ago by a speaker whose name I have long forgotten: 'Mission is the one thing the Church can do on earth that it cannot do in heaven.'

In thinking about defining mission further, however, Bosch's words of caution need to be taken into account:

> Ultimately, mission remains undefinable; it should never be incarcerated in the narrow confines of our own predelictions. The most we can hope for is to formulate some approximations of what mission is all about.[7]

In reaching towards 'approximations', can some criteria be set for the limits of mission or is it appropriate to ask when is the praxis of a Christian *not* mission in some sense?

31

If that is getting dangerously close to saying, 'if everything is mission, nothing is mission',[8] it may be more helpful to think of the Church's mission – given that this is its *raison d'être* – as a lens through which all activities can be seen and validated. For instance: will this Lent course enhance the lives of those attending such that they will be more aware of their Christian faith and themselves as bearers of the kingdom of God as they go about their daily lives tomorrow?

From this it can be deduced that everything a church does has or could have a missional aspect or bearing, even if indirectly. Mission could be said by extension to include everything an individual Christian does (and therefore mission is far more than a mode to switch in and out of, a programme to run or an event to stage). Neither the Church nor the individual Christian is operating in a social vacuum, and every action, attitude and statement has potential missional implications. Moltmann states that:

> Mission embraces all activities that serve to liberate man from his slavery in the presence of the coming God, slavery which extends from economic necessity to Godforsakenness. Evangelization is mission, but mission is not merely evangelization. In the missionary church the widow who does charitable works belongs to the same mission as the bishop who leads the church, or the preacher of the gospel.[9]

This wide, all-encompassing way of understanding mission is not universally accepted. In contrast to Bosch, Ferdinando argues for the need for a tighter definition of mission, reserved for specific activity by, and exclusive to, the Church. He identifies four approaches to mission as concentric circles, moving from broad and inclusive to increasingly narrow definitions. The outermost is *missio Dei* and he is concerned that the notion 'as used by some ... not only loses a word but also the very distinctiveness of God's work in Christ' as 'identifying mission as everything God wills to do in the world'. As this thereby potentially includes the action of non-Christians, whether consciously or not, it 'entails a potential marginalisation of the role of the church which is not the unique human vehicle of the *missio Dei'.*[10] His second and third categories narrow mission further. 'The Cultural Mandate', referencing Genesis 1:26-28, is 'the *church's* action in the world, rather than all that *God* does in the world'.[11] 'Social Action ... refers to the alleviation of human suffering and the elimination of injustice, exploitation and deprivation. It is thus specifically remedial and transformative, in a way not necessarily true of all that Christians do to glorify God in his world.'[12] Finally, as the 'innermost of the four concentric circles', comes 'Making Disciples of All Nations ... the essential, exclusive content of mission'. While he does not 'deny the importance of Christian social commitment', Ferdinando wants to 'reserve the word mission for the discipling of the peoples',[13] or, failing that, to invent a new term, such as 'apostolic mission'.

Matching Ferdinando's two innermost circles, Reformed theologian J. I. Packer defined mission as a task which is 'twofold':

First and fundamentally, it is the work of worldwide witness, disciple-making, and church-planting ...

Jesus Christ is to be proclaimed everywhere as God incarnate, Lord, and Savior; and God's authoritative invitation to find life through turning to Christ in repentance and faith ... is to be delivered to all mankind. ...

Second, all Christians, and therefore every congregation of the church on earth, are called to practice deeds of mercy and compassion, a thoroughgoing neighbor-love that responds unstintingly to all forms of human need as they present themselves.[14]

While deciding what does and does not count as 'mission' is, in part, an exercise in terminology, the danger with seeing mission solely as the exclusive action of the Church, rather than the Church's part in the action of God, lies in what is left out and thereby marginalised.

The appeal of holding to a narrower definition of mission is clear. It is much easier to identify what is and is not 'mission', and certain activities are valued above others accordingly, the extreme being overtly spiritual outreach activity addressed to a person's soul ranking above any social action or service to the body or mind. There is a safety in certainty, but I would argue that life – and the life of faith – are by nature messy and imprecise. Further, is there a correlation between a narrow view of mission, which compartmentalises certain activities as 'spiritual', and a dualistic non-consideration of lifestyle and cultural influences? As well as limiting mission to an occasional activity, this raises the question of Christian discipleship being reduced to being a 'devotional add-on to our "real lives"'[15] made up from predetermined life-choices, something I will return to later.

The particular notion of 'mission-with' which this book is about has arisen out of community engagement in a specific practical context. This requires a sufficiently wide and inclusive definition of mission to encompass such things as the missional implications or content of actions taken. These would include, as part of a 'mission-with' model, both ordinary actions in daily living in the locality, and actions alongside others in community engagement. But it runs the risk of being untidy and blurred at the edges as it becomes harder to define just what the missional aspect of some actions could be. Crucially, for praxis shared with others that could be said to be building *shalom*, this wide definition recognises that many of the facets of mission praxis in Bosch's list above – such as, service, justice, reconciliation – could be carried out by anyone of good will, and are not the exclusive preserve of Christians.

Shalom

The Hebrew word *shalom*[16] occurs more than 250 times in the Old Testament, and its Greek equivalent *eirene* appears more than 90 times in the New Testament. Linthicum notes that such heavy usage 'is a clear indication of how important a word it was – that it was a concept that permeated both Hebrew and early Christian society'.[17] Far richer in meaning than the direct translation of 'peace', *shalom* can be defined as a 'pervasive sense of well-being in personal, social, economic and political spheres'.[18] It is God's original creational intention which encompasses

35

'peace, soundness, wholeness, security and fullness of life, in which our relationships with God, each other and the wider creation are thriving'.[19]

The ministry of Jesus and His teaching about the kingdom of God demonstrate and reflect *shalom*.[20] Christine Sine describes the ministry of Jesus as 'giving breathtaking glimpses of that hoped for eternal shalom world where all will be healed, fed and provided for'.[21]

'Working for the Common Good' is one of the seven principles of Catholic Social Teaching. The Common Good is defined as 'the social conditions that enable human flourishing'. As these include physical, intellectual, moral and spiritual dimensions, there is a clear link to the *shalom* concept, but importantly with an emphasis on its communal and shared aspects.[22]

Aspects of this ideal seem to be wired into the human psyche, and aspiration to find or provide peace, healing and well-being turns up in all sorts of places. Manchester City Council regularly uses measures of 'well-being' in its policies and reports, defined as people 'satisfied with their lives'.[23] A 2006 Whitehall Wellbeing Working Group 'statement of common understanding of wellbeing for policy makers' has a lot in common with definitions of *shalom*:

> Wellbeing is a positive physical, social and mental state; it is not just the absence of pain, discomfort and incapacity. It arises not only from the action of individuals, but from a host of collective goods and relationships with other people. It requires that basic needs are met, that individuals have a sense of purpose, and that they feel able to achieve important

personal goals and participate in society. It is enhanced by conditions that include supportive personal relationships, involvement in empowered communities, good health, financial security, rewarding employment, and a healthy and attractive environment.[24]

Having described mission in broad terms as taking part in the *missio Dei* and building *shalom*, and therefore not restricted to the Church, it is important to recognise Ferdinando's concerns and agree that there are aspects which require Christian faith, such as verbal sharing of the gospel message and making disciples. It has been my experience, particularly in a sensitive multifaith context, that these 'mission-to' aspects, and those of 'mission-for', can be best and most effectively shared with humility and integrity when building on a relational foundation of mission praxis in another, less overt, form – 'mission-with'. They can therefore be reliant on this form, which should be valued equally as a part of the mission process.

'Mission-to' and 'mission-for'

These two expressions of mission can be seen as corresponding to the 'two tasks' of Packer's definition of mission described above. 'Mission-to' is concerned with taking something 'to' people, primarily overt sharing of the gospel message in evangelism and making disciples, though it could also apply to services and resources from a social action programme. 'Mission-for' is about doing something 'for' people. Here, the thought is primarily of providing for people's needs through social action, though it could also apply to providing for their spiritual needs. In both cases the missioner is the actor or giver and the people are the passive recipients, with the transaction being mostly in one direction. Both are about activity – projects and events which can be started and stopped. Goods, services and messages can be dispensed from a distance and completely at the discretion of the giver, who remains in charge of the process. Of course, this is in practice benign and well-meaning, but a sense of being 'done to' or of Christians as superior or judgemental 'do-gooders' – however mistaken – can result, as can issues of inferiority, dependency and passivity on the part of those on the receiving end.

In my experience and observation, this is how most mission praxis is done, and much good and positive work results. I am not advocating replacing 'mission-to' or 'mission-for'. However, triggered by my experience with Carisma and through reflection on my years living in the inner city, I began to ask if there is a further expression of mission beyond 'to' and 'for'. This would go alongside, complement, and could be a preparation for, 'mission-to and 'mission-for' praxis, which can benefit from an integrity earned through relationship based on identification, honesty and equality.

Seeing mission in terms of the *missio Dei*, as participating in God's action, rather than mission just being the Church's action, gives scope for a form of mission which is about fulfilling the *missio Dei*, particularly in building *shalom*, through action by Christians *with* others. To pick up Ferdinando's concentric circles, this is the outer circle, beyond the safe ground of the well-defined 'to' and 'for', but nonetheless also valid as mission and, while remaining of value in itself, a potential route into 'mission-to' and 'mission-for' praxis. The 'with' implies being alongside, identifying and in equal relationship, things that cannot be turned on and off, and so notions of mission praxis as episodic and being controlled by a provider have to be left behind.

'Mission-with' stage one: 'presence-among'

If 'mission-with' can be defined as 'presence-among' leading to 'project-praxis' (always in that order), 'presence-among', and the personal praxis that accompanies it, can be regarded as the first stage of 'mission-with'. A prerequisite of being involved 'with' people in the sense understood here and as described above, of partnering, sharing, giving and receiving and not only doing 'to' or 'for', is to be present among them in such a way that 'whatever happens to them, happens to me'.[25] In my own case this involved a relocation to a specific place through a sense of missional calling.

Personal praxis in daily life and interaction with other fellow residents in the neighbourhood follows as a consequence of being there – ordinary life in the context, but with a Christian distinctive. By 'distinctive' I mean an element of kingdom values present within the normal living of normal life – 'saltiness'[26] – changing the taste, preserving the good, making a difference – and not in the sense of separateness. As one gets to know and becomes known by the other residents, and particularly as that knowledge comes to include one's being a committed

Christian, then every action, attitude and response has potential as a missional act as it subtly refines, challenges or reinforces the other's view of what a Christian is and believes. This is the case with any relationship.

'Mission-with' stage two: 'project-praxis'

The second stage of 'mission-with', 'project-praxis', builds on the first as further action which arises in time as the specific, intentional response of a Christian to local issues, coming out of a concern shared with others and a desire to do something.

This is deeper than a concern arising from reading or hearing about an issue as it comes from being personally affected by it through living in the place where that issue is happening, where it is having an effect on people's lives, and you are one of those people. If the problem is the black ash coming from a nearby hospital incinerator chimney, as happened in our street in the late 1990s, then the concerned are those who live in the affected area and have the sooty deposit to contend with. In many ways the actions generated will be similar to what anyone else would do and with the same end: seeking to remedy the situation. Differences could lie in motivation, and in bringing Christian self-awareness. A general positive ethos, and desire to benefit the community, work for the common good and individual well-being, is one that a Christian can support and influence, as it can be seen as building *shalom*, both individually and corporately.

Whether taking the initiative oneself or joining in with what others may have started should make no difference.

The important values here are that everyone's praxis and contribution is equally valid, working and achieving together in partnership creates shared ownership and empowering, and the Christian can be one of those equal participants without having to be in control.

---

[1] David Bosch, *Transforming Mission: Paradigm Shifts in Theology of Mission* (Maryknoll, NY: Orbis, 1991), p.511.

[2] Bosch, *Transforming Mission*, p.16.

[3] Pietism's rediscovery of personal faith reintroduced mission within Europe, and Enlightenment expansionism and the advent of worldwide trade added a global dimension. Together these broke the Church out of the 'confines of "Christian society", which continually reproduces itself through infant baptism'. Jürgen Moltmann, *The Church in the Power of the Spirit: A Contribution to Messianic Ecclesiology* (London: SCM Press, 1977) p.9.

[4] Bosch, *Transforming Mission*, p.512.

[5] Bosch, *Transforming Mission*, p.10.

[6] Luke's introduction to the book of the Acts of the Apostles speaks of 'all that Jesus *began* to do and to teach' (my italics), implying strongly that there was more to do (Acts 1:1).

[7] Bosch, *Transforming Mission*, p.9.

[8] Stephen Neill's adage, quoted by Bosch, *Transforming Mission*, p.511. Stephen Neill, *Creative Tension* (London: Edinburgh House Press, 1959) p.81.

[9] Jürgen Moltmann, *The Church in the Power of the Spirit* (Minneapolis, MN: Augsburg Fortress) pp.10–11.

[10] Keith Ferdinando, 'Mission: A Problem of Definition', *Themelios* 33.1, 2008: pp.49, 50.

[11] Ferdinando, 'Mission', p.50.

[12] Ferdinando, 'Mission', p.52.

[13] Ferdinando, 'Mission', p.55.

[14] J. I. Packer, *Concise Theology: A Guide to Historic Christian Beliefs* (Carol Stream, IL: Tyndale House Publishers, 2001) pp.223–224.

[15] Tom Sine, 'Making It Real', *Sojourners Magazine*, January 2008, http://sojo.net/magazine/2008/01/making-it-real (accessed 4th October 2016).

[16] שלם 'Throughout the Heb. OT, *šālôm* covers well-being in the widest sense of the word.' Colin Brown, ed., *The New International Dictionary of New Testament Theology*, Vol. 2 (Carlisle: Paternoster, 1986), p.777. The New Testament equivalent, occurring 91 times, is εἰρήνη (*eirēnē*), also used to translate *šālôm* in the Septuagint (or LXX, a Greek translation of the Jewish scriptures from around 200BC). 'Both in form and content it stands firmly in the LXX and Heb.' Brown, p.780.

[17] Robert C. Linthicum, *Building a People of Power: Equipping Churches to Transform Their Communities* (Washington DC: Authentic, 2005), p.4.

[18] Donald B. Kraybill, *The Upside Down Kingdom*, 2nd edn (Scottdale, PA: Herald, 1990) p.200.

[19] Marijke Hoek, 'Yeasting the Public Debate with Good News', in Marijke Hoek, Jonathan Ingleby, Andy Kingston-Smith, Carol Kingston-Smith, eds., *Carnival Kingdom: Biblical Justice for Global Communities* (Gloucester: Wide Margin, 2013) p.209.

[20] 'This kingdom consists of the full reign of God in the world, a reign that restores right relationship among God, humanity, and the creation. Shalom finds its expression. A new order, divinely initiated, breaks into history. And in all this, the initial promises of covenant with creation and humanity become manifest in the life of the kingdom of God.' Wesley Granberg-Michaelson, 'Covenant and Creation', in Charles Birch, William Eaken and Jay B. McDaniel, eds., *Liberating Life: Contemporary Approaches in Ecological Theology* (Maryknoll, NY: Orbis, 1990) p.32.

[21] Christine Sine, 'Living Into God's Shalom World,' *Bible in TransMission*, Swindon: Bible Society, Spring 2008, p.1.

[22] 'This good is common because only together as a community, and not simply as isolated individuals, is it possible to enjoy, achieve, and spread this good.' Christopher Kaczor, 'Seven Principles of Catholic Social Teaching', in *Catholic Answers Magazine*, Vol. 18, no. 4, April 2007, http://www.catholic.com/magazine/articles/seven-principles-of-catholic-social-teaching (accessed 4th October 2016).

[23] For example: The Manchester Partnership, Manchester's State of The Wards Report, 2010-11, Manchester City Council, Issue 5, Sept. 2011, 2.5.4 Wellbeing, p.21.

[24] In Nicola Steuer and Nic Marks, *Local Wellbeing: Can We Measure It?* (London: The Young Foundation, 2008) p.8.

[25] Sheffield incomer Jane Grinonneau, quoted by John Vincent, *Hope from the City* (Peterborough: Epworth, 2000) p.131.

[26] From Jesus' teaching in several contexts: Matthew 5:13; Mark 9:50; Luke 14:34. Picked up by Paul: 'Be wise in the way you act towards outsiders; make the most of every opportunity. Let your conversation always be full of grace, seasoned with salt, so that you may know how to answer everyone' (Colossians 4:5-6).

Christian incomers

'Incomer' is a term used of an outsider coming into a place or community, described by the *Oxford Dictionary* as 'a person who has come to live in an area in which they have not grown up, especially in a close-knit rural community'.[1] It is used in the sense of immigrant or settler, and sometimes by indigenous people to denote someone who is 'not one of us'. There can be a number of reasons for becoming an incomer – family, economic, leisure – but they are usually to do with seeking to improve circumstances or enhance lifestyle.[2]

In our case, the deciding factor was one of Christian calling to a particular place and community, and it has resulted in what has been called a 'journey downward'.[3] I understand the use of 'downward' in the sense of how society measures people's worth by economic power, educational attainment and class, and our relative starting points, but I am uncomfortable with the overtones which could be seen as patronising. In kingdom terms, as a move towards those Jesus called 'blessed',[4] and who have much to teach me, then 'upward' also fits.

This journey might not always be the result of relocating, and the element of calling the only reason for it, but the inclusion of calling as a reason is the key feature in being a '*Christian* incomer'.

In telling my story the intention is not to put myself forward as a special case. I am one of a number of Christians from my church who, over the years, have chosen to move to and live in this part of Ardwick.[5] Additionally, across this city and country, and other cities and countries across the world, there are other fellow 'Christian incomers' who have made what is a deliberate downward move, most without any sort of fanfare.

We have deliberately chosen to not aspire to rise to the level where our economic potential as university-educated professionals would normally take us – big house, nice area, good schools, golf club and, more than likely, a lively church to be a part of (what I have heard called the Eleventh Commandment of the middle class: 'Thou Shalt Improve Thyself'). There is arguably nothing wrong with any of that in itself, except that as Christian incomers we have taken time out to ask God 'where?', not just 'what?' and responded to a sense of calling to be a part of this community, which has some 'issues'. There are plenty of *more* deprived areas in this city, but there are even more that are *less* deprived, especially out in the suburbs. There are, of course, also issues in the suburbs, as I have been reminded numerous times – just different ones. However, I wonder how many suburban dwellers would be willing to swap *their* issues for those of inner-city dwellers?

A fellow Christian incomer in another city sums it up well:

> We have tried to take the Bible seriously; it says go to the ends of the earth. One of those 'ends' in our society is most certainly the outer estate. We can't believe God wants all his name-owning salt and

light in the suburbs. We think it should take a special dispensation not to go and do likewise.[6]

A respondent in a recent Evangelical Alliance survey into Christian attitudes to poverty commented:

> Most Christians seem to move into the nicest area they can afford to get away from anti-social behaviour and working class people. Then they come to church and talk about wanting to reach everyone.[7]

A Christian calling and decision to live here, and not where most of our peer group gravitates, challenges the assumption that that is what everyone does. There are some parallels with the classic calling to overseas missionary work, and further parallels once in situ, such as learning to function in a different culture. Calling and culture as crucial aspects of our story will be among the topics reflected on below.

However, I am not aware of any incomers I know having 'gone home' on furlough. This *is* home. It is, first of all, ordinary life. I have no particular sense of this being special or heroic and I am fairly certain other Christian incomers would share that view.

It is this understanding of calling, including 'where' as well as, or even before, 'what', that is the foundation on which 'mission-with' has been developed.

[1] http://oxforddictionaries.com/definition/english/incomer (accessed 4th October 2016).

[2] My wife's hometown, Whitstable in Kent, has in recent years seen an influx of incomers from London buying weekend and holiday homes. This has affected the town's economy, in positive and negative ways. They are known locally as 'DFLs' (Down From London).

[3] John Vincent, *Radical Jesus: The Way of Jesus Then and Now* (Sheffield: Ashram Press, 2006) p.83.

[4] Luke 6:20.

[5] What is different about my case is that my day job has been that of a 'full-time Christian worker', currently as part of Urban Presence, a charity set up for the express purpose of encouraging a stronger Christian presence in areas such as this. A part of that work is to encourage theological reflection on mission and ministry praxis in inner-city contexts, so that could be said to be good reason to tell my particular story as an example of 'incoming', and also try to reflect on it and draw out the theological implications.

[6] Andy Dorton, 'On the Estate', in Michael Eastman and Steve Latham, eds., *Urban Church: A Practitioner's Resource Book* (London: SPCK, 2004) p.63.

[7] Evangelical Alliance, *21st Century Evangelicals: Good News for the poor?* (London: Evangelical Alliance, 2015) p.22.

Welcome to Ardwick, Manchester

Manchester is one of ten boroughs that make up Greater Manchester, the largest conurbation in the United Kingdom outside of London, with a population approaching 2.75 million. The Borough of Manchester, the largest of the ten by population, has just over half a million people, most of whom live in the inner-city areas which encircle the city centre. Population density across the borough is the highest in England.

Manchester historian Alan Kidd describes this inner-city ring as a 'poverty belt' which dates back to the rapid industrial expansion of early Victorian times, stubbornly persisting to the present day. Deprivation 'is more widespread than in any other UK city and many neighbourhoods display levels of social and economic deprivation substantially above the national averages'.[1]

Despite many advances made by the city in recent years as an often imaginative council has, with some success, sought to rebrand Manchester as a European city, the persistence of deprivation has remained an embarrassment as the city's position 'remains consistently high across all measures of deprivation'.[2]

One author, referencing the famous description of deprivation in Manchester by Engels in 1844, comments that:

the correlation between the worst housing, the greatest poverty and the shortest life expectancy is painfully evident from the statistics. The thresholds may have been raised, but the pattern is one that would have been familiar to ... Friedrich Engels, almost two centuries ago.[3]

The 'inner-south' is Manchester City Council's designation for part of that belt. It contains large amounts of housing – mostly social and private rented with some owner-occupied – local amenities such as shops and schools, recreation areas in the form of several city parks, and a small amount of light industry. It is intersected by a strip along one of the main arterial roads containing, going from north to south, part of the Manchester Metropolitan University campus, the main campus of Manchester University, the largest in the United Kingdom, a recently rebuilt hospital complex which is now the largest in Europe, and 'Curry Mile', an area with a high concentration of Asian restaurants, food shops and other businesses that attracts visitors from across Greater Manchester and beyond. This is one of the expressions of a rich ethnic mix across the area.

Part of the inner-south is Ardwick Ward which is immediately south of the city centre, and we live in the Chorlton-on-Medlock district of the ward. After four years in a top-floor flat at the northern end of Brunswick council estate, in May 1983 we moved to our present address in Upper West Grove, Chorlton-on-Medlock, and close to the southern end of the estate.

A separate village before the Industrial Revolution, Ardwick became a wealthy suburb of Manchester in the nineteenth century (and known as such by social commentators Charles Dickens and Friedrich Engels), and home to famous Victorian families such as the Peels, the Gaskells and the Pankhursts.[4] As Manchester continued to grow, Ardwick became heavily industrialised and filled with factories, railways and back-to-back terraced houses. As decline set in, these were to form part of the extensive slums that were cleared after the Second World War in a determined effort by the council at regeneration. Unfortunately, owing to haste, false economies, design errors, and insufficient consideration to things such as provision of adequate local amenities, much of the new housing has since had to be refurbished or, in some cases, replaced.

In recent years several PFIs (Private Finance Initiatives) have begun a fresh wave of demolition, rebuilding and refurbishment of houses mostly less than 40 years old. A new characteristic of these schemes where they are in inner areas close to the city centre is a mix of different sizes and styles of houses and apartments, some for purchase, some for rent, hoping to attract an influx of more affluent residents, creating a mixed-income community, as the demand for city-centre dwellings bulges into the inner city. In the case of Ardwick, the new Grove Village, next to Chorlton-on-Medlock, has been created within an estate built in the 1970s as an attempt to solve a high crime rate by dilution, replacing a third of the houses with new mixed housing and refurbishing the rest. Another PFI is now underway on the northern end of the estate – Brunswick. One of the first areas to be refurbished includes the block of flats we used to live in: also the area closest to the city centre.

This half-century of building, repairing, demolishing and rebuilding, with the disruption of moving residents or them having to live in building sites, has had a cumulative destabilising effect, not conducive to people feeling settled, secure or rooted in their communities.

As a part of the inner-city ring, Ardwick Ward features consistently in the lower ends of the various Indices of Multiple Deprivation and has become known for its poor health statistics. 'Ardwick has the most severe health related deprivation within the central wards, ranked within the most deprived 1% of wards in England.'[5] 'Life expectancy at birth is lower in the ward than in Manchester as a whole and significantly lower than life expectancy in England.'[6]

Despite the statistics and the conditions they describe, the modern inner-south area of Manchester is a far cry from the squalor of Engels' time, and the positives of the area, to which I can testify from more than 35 years of personal experience, are many, not least the friendliness and good humour of the majority of the people. The vibrancy of the mix of many cultures gives a richness to the area, shown particularly in food and festivals. Our children have grown up in these streets and attended a local school with many different countries of origin. We feel this has given them an advantage over young people in other more monocultural areas of the city or country as they make their way in our pluralist, multicultural society. Not something they can get an A level in, but ultimately more valuable.

But I'm getting ahead of myself...

[1] Alan Kidd, *Manchester,* 4th edn (Lancaster: Carnegie, 2006) p.247.

[2] Manchester Partnership, *State of the City Report 2011/2012,* p.26.

[3] Stuart Hylton, *A History of Manchester* (Chichester: Phillimore, 2003) p.232. Friedrich Engels was a German socialist philosopher whose classic work *The Condition of the Working Class in England* (1845) was based on observations from several years living in Manchester.

[4] Robert Peel was an MP and Prime Minister who founded the first police force; Elizabeth Gaskell was an author; Emmeline Pankhurst was the leader of the Suffragette movement, campaigning for votes for women.

[5] Manchester City Council, *Ardwick Local Plan,* 2008, p.87.

[6] Manchester City Council, *Ardwick Ward Profile 2011/12,* 2011, p.23. 'A child born today in some parts of Manchester will live twelve years less than one born in, say, Surrey.' Tony Lloyd, Police and Crime Commissioner and Interim Mayor for Greater Manchester. Interview, 21st September 2016.

Part Two

Where – Presence: Story and Reflection

With is the most important word in theology.[1]

---

[1] Samuel Wells, *A Nazareth Manifesto: Being With God* (John Wiley & Sons, Chichester, 2015) p.231.

Introduction: Northern Ireland

I grew up in Northern Ireland, living through the early years of 'The Troubles', in what I discovered when they began was a 'mixed' suburban estate. Before that, what religion my friends and their families were had not occurred to me. Looking back, having both Protestant and Catholic friends growing up probably saved me from imbibing much of the bigotry that has poisoned that society for so long.

Northern Ireland is the most religious part of the United Kingdom and I was brought up to go to church and Sunday school. It was something just about all my friends and neighbours also did, but in many cases, including my own, it was just something you did on a Sunday, with little, if any, relevance to the rest of the week or to life. As soon as I could, I stopped going. So it came as a bit of a surprise when, in 1972 while still at school, I made a Christian commitment through being invited to hear globe-trotting American evangelist Arthur Blessitt who was passing through Belfast. A friend had made a commitment a few months earlier; I couldn't really understand what he was on about when he tried to 'witness' to me, but I could see some changes in his behaviour, so went along with him, and suddenly it made sense. Well, enough to make a decision to follow Jesus: I am still trying to work out what

I let myself in for. I started going to church again, but a different one.

Arthur Blessitt left behind a quite a number of enthusiastic new converts, and some of us were given use of a room in a building owned by an evangelistic organisation in the nearby town of Lisburn and began to do street outreach on Saturday nights. We found a pile of gospel tracts in a cupboard and started to give them out. One was called 'Booze' and we figured we could take it into the pubs. Thankfully, no one in those pubs read what they'd been given or we may not have got out in one piece. It was only when we got back someone realised that a leaflet with the opening line, 'Drink is a distilled damnation, the devil in solution' and a harsh fundamentalist theology was not the sort of thing we wanted to distribute, and we binned them. This was an early encounter with a form of fundamentalist evangelical Protestantism that was quite strong in Northern Ireland. There were more to follow. It was anti-Catholic, judgemental and came across as superior and strident in its certainty of being right, and I did not like it.

A few years later I went to Queen's University Belfast to study theology – another change of direction that led from my new-found faith. At that time this conservative evangelicalism was dominant in the Christian Union and, though less virulent, I still struggled to relate to it.

The CU had a one-week spring-term mission every three years. This occurred in my first year, by which time I had already sampled the Christian Union and been put off by its lack of involvement with student life. It seemed to be a little subculture of its own – except when it went into 'mission-mode'. I recall overhearing this comment on the steps of the Student Union building during the mission week: 'Let's go and eat somewhere else – the Christians are in this week.'

During the rest of the year, members of the CU would go into the Student Union building one evening a week when they had hired a room for their regular meeting. Some would go into the refectory for lunch and sit together. Their table was easy to spot – it was the one where the occupants would pause briefly to rub their eyebrows just before starting to eat. Few if any went up a floor to eat in the snack bar, though there was a 'Snack Bar Witness Team' – a few brave souls who, after an earnest prayer, would venture in to accost students trying to eat a burger in peace, with opening lines such as (and I can remember it precisely from my one week as a member), 'Do you know what sin is?' None went to the two licensed bars.

During mission week, however, Christians were all over the Student Union like a rash – giving out leaflets, putting up posters, hiring rooms for daily lunchtime and evening meetings, trying to persuade people to go in. A few did, but others, such as the two who I overheard, just gave the Union a wide berth all week.

Not through any great spiritual revelation, but instead the need to supplement our income, in our second year a friend and I took part-time jobs in the Student Union. We ran the late-night catering stand. This sold snacks and soft drinks to students in the evening through to the early hours when the two bars emptied. Through this work we got to know all of the Union staff, such as the porters, refectory and shop workers, and the student officers, plus,

57

of course, our 'regulars'. While we didn't hide the fact that we were Christians, we also didn't broadcast it blatantly – we just got on with our work and kept it friendly to all and good-natured with the tipsy.

One day we were summoned by the manager of the Union – a permanent non-student post – who wanted to know why for the first time in his experience the late-night catering was operating at a profit! Quite simply it was because we were running it honestly. We told him we were Christians so 'losing' a few pounds of the takings or 'borrowing' a tray of colas for a party were not the sort of thing we did. Word spread. During our time working in the Union we had prayer requests, such as from a porter whose wife was ill, and a number of long conversations with people who were relaxed and on their own territory. Plus a bit of banter from the drunks along the lines of, 'If you're a Christian, you should *give* me a burger!' Looking back, it was a formative experience.

During my fourth and final year, Christian Union mission time came round again. Independently of the CU, I was able to use my contacts in the Student Union to stage two lunchtime concerts as part of the mission, actually *in* the refectory and snack bar. No problems trying to invite people in – they were there already! Our home-grown band went down well, though a few objected, and that started a lively debate which featured on the front page of the student newspaper. I was later told this was the first time the CU mission had ever had an editorial mention in the newspaper.

As an unintended by-product of needing a job, this was an early lesson for me about the potential difference in effectiveness between two approaches to mission. One a hit-and-run strategy from a safe and unengaged distance, and the other a positive witness built up in a natural and relational way through a contrast in attitude and practice in a context of working alongside others.

Coming to Manchester... and staying

After graduating in 1978 I came to Manchester for a year as a postgraduate student, as the first half of training to be a probation officer. Or so I thought at the time.

On my first Sunday I attended 'Brunswick', an Anglican church situated on Brunswick council housing estate in Ardwick near the university. Not that I was, or am, Anglican: I had decided from my experience and observations of life in Northern Ireland that denominational affiliation – as distinct from belonging to a local expression of Church – was unbiblical and more trouble than it was worth. The normal practice for Christian students arriving in a city was to spend several weeks 'sampling' the various churches before settling in one. For me, one visit to Brunswick was enough. It was friendly, informal, and close by.

I got drawn into the life of the church and its mission to its parish, which mostly comprised council housing. I began to learn about life on the estate and got to know some of the residents, for many of whom 'church', 'God', 'Jesus' and anything related was an almost total irrelevance.

I remember speaking to a man who genuinely thought that the church building was a swimming pool. It is a modern building, and the side of it he would have passed on his way to and from the local shops has few windows and does not afford a view of the foot-high white plastic letters: 'Brunswick Parish Church'. This ignorance of Church and what it is about was in marked contrast to what I had been used to in Northern Ireland, where Church and 'The Gospel' had a much higher profile. If anything, this had the effect of inoculating many people, whereas at least on Brunswick estate things were more clear-cut. A local young person who had been attending our youth work had a Gideon New Testament at home that he had been given at school and decided to read it. 'I used that bit at the front that tells you what to read if you're feeling sad or lonely. It said Romans 8. I turned to page 8 and I couldn't find any Romans anywhere.' This would not have happened in Belfast.

Brunswick's minister was Martin Gooder. With his wife, Carol, he had committed to serve in this area long-term and had already been there for 12 years (they were to remain until the early 1990s), guiding the church through a period of extensive demolition and rebuilding across the area. This included the new church building, opened in 1974, which Martin helped design.

Through Martin's teaching and example I began to learn about inner-city life and ministry. Although the old slums had to go, with them had gone much of any sense of community, as residents had been summarily dispersed, many of them some distance away to overspill estates such as Hattersley and Wythenshawe's Benchill. The new houses were filled randomly with people from across the city who were expected to create community from scratch.

The houses were better, but loneliness, deprivation and poor health persisted.

Martin Gooder's theological basis for inner-city mission and ministry, seeing it in missionary and incarnational terms, was to prove influential for me in learning about mission as being a witness and presence in a community, and pivotal in a growing sense of call to the inner city.[1]

Such was his clarity of vision that Gooder actively discouraged people from joining for what might be different reasons. Church was not primarily for the comfort of the members: it was there first for the cure of souls in the parish.[2]

Owing to the proximity of the university, each autumn a fresh wave of students would turn up to check out the church (as I had done), with some deciding to settle there. Martin and Carol were welcoming and pastoral, but also very clear that the primary mission of the church was to the local estate, and students would be expected to join in with that in some way. This challenge was made with a smile and a post-service showing of 'The Brunswick Story' – slides of the recent history of the area, demolition, new houses and the new church building.

> We are asking that you should join us in attempting to build a church which is culturally unsuited to your own interests – in which at times you will feel uncomfortable so that the local people may feel at home. ... Our policy therefore is to discourage people from coming here, if they come for the wrong reasons. ... It is essential that our leaders and potential leaders ... understand clearly all the issues involved and have sufficient missionary

commitment to sacrifice their own interests for the sake of the people of Brunswick.[3]

On a few occasions, feeling too many students were coming to Brunswick, Martin had no qualms about encouraging some to move to other inner-city churches where their presence would be much more useful. This generous willingness to share and give away was something I admired him for.

Staying in Manchester

As the months of that first year in Manchester passed, I began to feel increasingly uncomfortable about my plans to apply for the second year of probation training which would entail moving to another city. I wanted to stay in Manchester, and one day in March 1979 I tore up the application forms I had for courses. Reflecting back, I think I was feeling the beginnings of a call to the inner city, but at the time it was more a case of knowing what I did not want to do.

Not long afterwards I was offered a job for a year at Brunswick Church. Martin had found funding to employ someone to take on some administrative jobs, freeing him to visit other urban churches and lead missions or give training. While he was away our curate Pete Hobson would be in charge.

This role was to begin in September. Meanwhile I completed the last few months of my course, spent the summer working as a musician in Holland (continuing something I had done back in Belfast) and started seeing a pretty redhead called Judith I had been getting to know.

Judith was from the seaside town of Whitstable in Kent and had come to Manchester University in 1976 to train as a speech therapist. Her background, like mine, was middle/upper-working-class, and she had also got involved at Brunswick Church and in the local area.

The year working at Brunswick involved things like attempting to fix holes in the church roof, producing the monthly *Brunswick Broadsheet* on an ancient Gestetner duplicator (with a page count in excess of a million), getting supplies from the cash and carry and a number of other behind-the-scenes jobs. As part of the staff team I got to work closely with Martin, Carol, Pete and his wife, Sue, and even went along on some of the mission trips, usually to help with music. I learned more about inner-city ministry and lived in 'Barnabas', one of the two church community houses.

These had been bought several years previously to house several members who wanted to live locally but would not be able to qualify for council housing, which at the time made up just about all the housing stock in the parish. 'Barnabas' and 'Timothy' were 'as near as possible' compromises just off the estate. Martin Gooder wrote about those of us who felt a calling to live locally:

> Some of the students had caught the vision of the need for involvement in inner-city ministry. We thank God for those who deliberately looked for jobs in the Manchester area after graduating in order to play a part in our teams. We have had to pray and work hard to find housing for such people in a basically council housing estate. We have had two community houses on the edge of the parish. Others

have lived in deck-access housing which the Council deemed as unfit for families. Still others have made considerable financial sacrifices to buy houses in the small areas of private housing which have recently been built.[4]

Through the year my sense of calling to live in this area grew stronger, and I decided to put my name down for a council flat in the parish on Brunswick estate. This was towards the end of 1979. Judith shared this call to inner-city Manchester and we had got engaged (at a speed we would never recommend to our own children).

Lockton Court

I did not have enough points to get a council flat. However, as there were several people willing to take my place in 'Barnabas', a letter to the council led to an offer of a single-bedroom flat on the top floor of Lockton Court. This is an eight-storey block at the north end of the estate, overlooking the inner ring road, and one of the deck-access[5] blocks referred to by Martin Gooder above which the council had deemed unfit for families. The previous tenant had left the flat in a bad state, which on first viewing made my stomach turn, especially the smell from the rubbish bags piled up on the balcony (the walk to the rubbish chute must have been too far). I initially felt a bit uncertain. Was this a mistake? Should I have waited for something better, or just cleaner? A stronger feeling was that this was an answer to prayer – I felt a call to the inner city, I had asked God to make it possible for me to move onto the estate, and here it was.

Waiting on the council's Direct Works to come and clean it up would have taken several weeks, so with the help of a work-party of friends from church, we did it ourselves and I had moved in by late January 1980. My first home of my own, and my first time living on my own.

The block was one of three on the estate, all single-bedroom. The flat had some good points. A large main room with huge windows at one end with a great view looking south-west over the city. The kitchen also had a view north-east which on a clear day included the distant hills behind Oldham. Being right by the ring road meant traffic noise, but I got used to that surprisingly quickly. The flat had underfloor heating which didn't work and I never got fixed as it was known to be notoriously expensive, and besides, being on the top floor I reckoned I got some benefit from the floors below. The location was great: five minutes' walk from the main railway station, Piccadilly, and less than ten minutes to the city centre. The church was a few minutes' walk in the other direction across the estate.

I continued with my job at the church, along with more events and concerts, and around Easter got an offer from Youth for Christ (YFC) to join with two other musicians in a band that would work mostly in schools, beginning in September. Judith graduated as a speech therapist in the summer and accepted an offer of a job in Salford. We got married on 27th September, and 69 Lockton Court became our first home together. Ironically, just as we began living in an inner-city area, I started a job that would take me all over the country, and occasionally further, for weeks at a time. But the base was here.

How did Judith feel about being left alone in an inner-city estate council flat? As she recalls, it may have been youthful optimism but mostly life was pretty normal despite the reputation of the area, and she has no memories of being frightened when I was away. She was at work all day when we were in the flat and there were neighbours nearby and a kind of security system at the main door to the block. There were also church friends living locally. And, of course, familiarity helps. By the time Judith moved into the flat she had already been a member of Brunswick Church for four years and involved in ministry such as Friends of the Flats,[6] so she was known by many in the local area.

My job with YFC took me to a wide variety of local situations and gave me experience of different, if predominantly evangelical, churches, working alongside them on periods of mission. However, even in that role it quickly became apparent that our effectiveness depended to a large extent on the degree of local ongoing missional lifestyle present in the context we were coming into. Through this itinerant work I was becoming more aware of the contrast between churches in suburban areas and those in inner-urban and overspill areas, which as a rule were smaller and often tended to struggle. Looking back now, I can see that seeds were being sown.

The majority of the flats contained just one person, as was the case with quite a few of the houses and other flats on the estate, making many people isolated as there seemed to be little neighbourly spirit.

Sometimes this was evidenced in quite dramatic ways. I remember going to a flat in another of the blocks in response to a request for prayer as the owner thought it was haunted. The issue turned out to be guilt feelings. A neighbour had been found dead in his flat just after Christmas. It was reckoned he had been there for some time, as it was the smell that finally raised the alarm. If someone had just looked through the letterbox, his body had been quite visible in the hall.

Neighbours on our floor included two elderly sisters in separate flats at either end, an ex-tank driver who had fought in the war in North Africa and Italy, a lovely Catholic lady, and a mysterious man we only saw a few times. The only other couple were retired Glaswegians who lived next door. Despite many years in Manchester, the wife often had to translate her husband's still broad dialect for us. Then there was Mrs Sargeant, an elderly widow we already visited through the church's Friends of the Flats scheme. Quite a bit of her coffee made with sterilised milk ended up in her plant pots when she wasn't looking. Mrs S had lost her ring finger a few years before when falling off a stool she was standing on to close a window. The finger had remained in the window frame. She put it in an envelope and walked to A and E, about half a mile away, and took her place in the queue. By the time she was seen it was too late to do anything.

There was a flat on the third floor with a red bulb in the kitchen, which never had its curtains drawn. A young couple below us had violent arguments, once involving throwing a TV out of the window, and we called the police on several occasions. Sometimes there were bloodstains, or abandoned underwear, as well as the more usual litter.

Apart from Mrs S, it was rare to be invited into a neighbour's flat. Most interaction was on the shared balcony our front doors opened on to, or waiting for the lift. We realised going for meals or coffee was a middle-class thing, among white British at least: in some Asian and Muslim cultures, hospitality is important. In one flat we were in I noticed a large bookcase that contained one book and quite a few videos. Our bookcase contained books. We asked Martin Gooder if we should move our books into the bedroom. His reply was: 'No. You need to be yourselves. If you try to be something you are not, people will sense your discomfort. You can only go so far in identifying with local people. A lot of people around here, it's not that they can't read, it's more that they don't read. This is why we do lots of visual stuff in the services. It's not that one way is better or worse, just different.' The books stayed put.

> You cannot avoid being who you are. You cannot run away from what your birth, upbringing, education, church allegiance, reading habits, cultural interests, friends and peer-groups have made you. You are a rich person not a poor person. ... But you can do something. You can decide whether you are going to put yourself in a situation where all those tendencies and elements within your make-up are going to be confirmed, protected and exaggerated – or whether you are going to put yourself in a situation where these tendencies and elements are going to be questioned, exposed and curtailed.[7]

I was away with the band in July 1981 when the Moss Side riots took place. Over the phone, Judith told me of seeing groups of people from our estate heading across to Moss Side and hearing the noise and seeing the flames from her eighth-floor vantage point. The local buzz was that our area was not quite as organised as Moss Side (and, some added, the shops were not worth looting), so we just joined in over there. By an incredible piece of foresight, or maybe godly insight, our church had already organised 'A Festival for Brunswick' to take place in early September. This proved a timely and positive response to the riots and included a successful family carnival day on the local primary school sports field.

> People were encouraged into involvement in an event they'd previously shown no interest in, and *they enjoyed it*! Set against the backcloth of July riots (Moss Side only a mile away) this was doubly rewarding to see, and a pointer to the whole estate that it can be otherwise![8]

We learned about the frustrations of being a council tenant in several ways. One missed rent payment, caused by our bank missing a standing order payment, resulted in a repossession notice. This arrived while I was working away, and was an intimidating and frightening experience for Judith. We were able to sort it out, but we did wonder, and challenged a council officer: if this had caused us such a shock, what effect would it have had on elderly or more vulnerable tenants?

The council did not always move so fast. Lockton Court had a flat roof and was generally not in great repair. The hole in the roof right over the cooker in our kitchen took eleven months to fix. We heard stories from neighbours of broken toilets that took weeks to repair, or of other faults that they did not bother to report or attempted to fix themselves. It was not uncommon for people to lose their tempers in the council's Neighbourhood Office, venting their frustration on a council worker usually with no personal responsibility for the problem.

On one occasion when I was waiting to be seen, a man who had been having a heated discussion with a member of staff suddenly picked up the heavy metal stand the queuing rope was attached to and smashed it against the glass twice. The glass was armoured so did not break, but the staff on the other side still leapt in all directions. He then set the stand down, turned to the queue and apologised, sat on the floor and burst into tears. A few minutes later the police arrived.

A person on a low wage or benefits, with a fragile self-esteem, and a history of being ignored or fobbed off by 'them' (whether perceived or actual), will learn to minimise further future disappointment by lowering their aspirations and altering their expectations. When dealing with the authorities the default will be to assume the answer will be 'no'. Over the years many have described themselves to us as 'stupid'. Sometimes an inability to articulate the frustration will explode into violence. During our time living in Lockton Court as council tenants we grew to understand and share the feelings of frustration and resignation. However, because of our background, it seemed we were better equipped than many to deal with the council, with more confidence and awareness of our rights giving us a (mostly) polite but firm attitude, whether for an issue we had, or advocating for a neighbour. It still took eleven months to fix the roof.

The lift

One of our dealings with the council concerned the lifts. There were two: a large one which served the even-numbered floors, and a tiny one which served the odd-numbered floors. Some of our elderly neighbours would only use the big lift as the little one gave them claustrophobia. So when it started to break down every few days, each time requiring the fire brigade to come and rescue whoever was inside, many of them took to using the stairs the whole way or, in some cases, just would not go out. Individual letters or complaints at the Neighbourhood Office brought no response from the council. After several weeks of breakdowns, Judith and I decided to put together a petition and take it round all the doors. Just about everyone signed and the petition was sent to the council, with a letter, also copied to our MP, Gerald Kaufmann, local councillor, the *Manchester Evening News* and the local vicar, Martin Gooder. We had letters from the MP and councillor, promising to investigate, and an article in the newspaper. 'Anguished old age pensioners living in a Manchester block of flats are demanding action to keep their lift working before tragedy strikes ...'[9] The lift was fixed within a week.

Beyond a sense that it might have a side effect of helping us to get to know some of the other residents better with a view to inviting them to the Carol Service, we had no particular sense at the time that our lift campaign was a missional activity in itself. It was a human response to an issue that was causing all of us problems. Our missional activity amounted to the delivery of the church's monthly *Brunswick Broadsheet* and any conversations that came out of it. At this time, I was clearly still operating on a 'mission-to' basis, with some 'mission-for' through Friends of the Flats or as needs presented themselves. Unknown to me at the time, but reflecting back now – given that it was an action that would improve the well-being, or *shalom*, of the residents – by the wider definition of mission I have since adopted, getting the lift repaired was a missional act in and of itself.[10] Additionally, some years later I was to realise that my response to this problem of the council's intransigence was an unconscious piece of 'Community Organising', if only in getting the other residents involved by signing their names – everything else we did 'for' them rather than 'with'. More of this was to follow, but with a better understanding of the wider missional application and the value of the activity in itself and not just as a means to a spiritual end.

Reflections on Lockton Court

'What with all the stuff on the news, I thought there would only be about three buildings and 12 of you left.' This was a comment by a visiting musician at a concert I attended in Belfast back in the seventies. He went on to say that his first sight of the city as he came out of York Road station confirmed this impression, as the area by the station at that time was being cleared for redevelopment! I have spoken many times since with people this side of the Irish Sea who have had similar impressions of life in Northern Ireland when 'The Troubles' were at their height. This is because the normal things in life, which continue on most of the time, are not what gets reported. My dad travelling into work each morning never made the news. The few occasions when his journey was disrupted by an explosion or shooting would have been reported. However, also not reported was 'normal' life in many parts of the city – usually poor – where the rival communities lived in ghettoes in close proximity. There a man going to work, if he had a job to go to, would think nothing of the fact that his route would take him round and not through certain streets. People adapt and readjust quickly and 'normality', slightly tweaked, returns. For the most part, this is a good thing, as life has to continue. The danger, however, is to lose sight of the issues and injustices behind the circumstances requiring the readjustments.

In a similar way, what makes the headlines about the inner city are the stories of crime, ASBOs (Anti-Social Behaviour Orders), benefit fraud and racism. Not deemed newsworthy (and why should it be?) is that most of the time in our inner-city location we were living ordinary lives doing ordinary things. We went to our jobs, shopped for food, went to church, and visited friends. Occasionally something would occur that would remind us of where we were, but we soon became virtually oblivious to things like the unsanitary or exotic aromas in the lift. Judith's colleagues at work were a bit puzzled as to why she did not live in a 'nicer' area. Our parents were a bit perplexed.

Gradually we grew aware of some of the dynamics of where we were: this was not suburbia.

We learned a lot during those few years in Lockton Court and, looking back, the beginnings of 'mission-with' were forming. Thanks to the teaching at Brunswick Church, we had no great pretensions about heroically and sacrificially sweeping in to help these unfortunate people, who would be so grateful for our presence among them as we fixed all their problems. First and foremost we were to *be* there, living alongside as neighbours.

---

[1] I will look at Martin Gooder's theology more closely below.

[2] 'The church is the church only when it exists for others.' David Bosch, *Transforming Mission*, p.375. This is reminiscent of the quotation attributed to the former Archbishop of Canterbury, William Temple: 'The Church is the only society that exists for the benefit of those who are not its members.'

[3] Martin L. Gooder, *The Brunswick Papers*, Manchester: self-published, 1988, p.160.

[4] Gooder, *Brunswick Papers*, p.70.

[5] In deck access flats the front door of each flat opens on to a shared balcony that runs along each floor, leading to stairs and lifts.

[6] The Friends of the Flats scheme offered a weekly visit from one of a team of volunteers. Many took this offer up and some came into the life of the church as a result.

[7] Vincent, *Radical Jesus*, p.81.

[8] Peter Hobson, 'A Festival for Brunswick', *Mainstream*, 14, September 1983, p.13, http://www.biblicalstudies.org.uk/pdf/ma instream/14.pdf (accessed 4th October 2016).

[9] 'Old folk live in fear of faulty lift', *Manchester Evening News*, July 1982.

[10] 'Mission is a multi-faceted ministry, in respect of witness, service, justice, healing, reconciliation, liberation, peace, evangelism, fellowship, church planting, contextualisation and much more.' Bosch, *Transforming Mission*, p.512.

The Groves (there's no place like home)

By 1983 we were wondering about starting a family. Our flat was not intended for children, and the council would not let them to families. However, to get enough points for something larger in the area required having one child with another expected. A small number of new private houses were being built on another part of the estate, but they were very small and beyond our means. Martin told us about The Groves, tucked away between two roads running along one side of the estate and the closest bit of older private housing. It turned out these were five streets of terraced houses that had survived the demolition of the 1960s and 1970s thanks partly to their good condition but also because their residents had campaigned for them to be left alone. We had a look and saw one house had a For Sale sign. Though still not huge, it was much larger than the new-builds on the estate and around half the price. We liked it, and after some dithering, decided to buy.

This felt very grown up and a bigger step. I can remember sitting on the floor in the empty living room and saying to God, 'I think this is where we are meant to be and we intend to move here. If this is not your leading, then please stop us!' On the basis of Isaiah 30:21, we did not hear a voice saying, 'This is the way; walk in it,' and assumed in faith that we had not turned to the right or the left, and were moving on the right path.

On hearing that we were going from renting to mortgaging, the response from well-meaning relatives or friends was that they were glad we had moved on to the 'property ladder'. They were relieved that we were doing the sensible thing, moving on from our inner-city council flat and investing in property. The relief faded when they saw where we had moved to, but implied behind the comments about our house as a first step on said ladder was the assumption that we would eventually move again to somewhere 'better'. To date we are still on that step. It has to be added that once family and friends understood our motives for coming here (whether or not they agreed or shared our values) they quickly got over their initial shock and have been encouraging and supportive.

The overriding factor in our decision to move to The Groves was the location, being within the same area and close to where the church met. A lesser factor was my low income at the time; we got the mortgage on the strength of Judith's job as a speech therapist. At that time, going from renting to the then popular endowment mortgage, our monthly outgoings actually went down. Though we could probably, with help from parents, have exercised an option to move to a more expensive house further out, an option many of our neighbours would not have, we also did not want to tie up too much of our income in mortgage payments, and this became more crucial a couple of years later when Judith stopped working.

We moved in May 1983, a distance of about a mile and still within Ardwick Ward, and have lived in Upper West

Grove since. Being an older, terraced street rather than a deck-access block of flats, The Groves has a very different feel to Lockton Court, and the mix of neighbours is wider, including African, Caribbean, Asian and Irish. Many of the houses are owned by a social housing association, some by individual landlords, who tend to have students, and the rest are owner-occupiers. There are 142 houses in five streets, North, South, East, West and Upper West Groves, which form a rough capital 'A' shape. On two sides are the new-build council houses of the 1970s.

The area's old, official name is Chorlton-on-Medlock (many of us like the posh-sounding hyphenation). Chorlton-on-Medlock is also known as 'Little Ireland' owing to the number of Irish immigrants that settled here over the years up to the 1960s. Some of our Irish neighbours are still with us. One of them is a charming and twinkly-eyed retired widower who supplements his pension by painting the exteriors of many of the houses on our street. He has been in Manchester since the 1950s but his brogue remains very strong. He is a well-known and much-loved neighbour who welcomes people from every culture.

Our streets are very close to Manchester's main hospital complex, which is a major local employer, and includes St Mary's, where our three children were born. Recently there has been a major redevelopment of the whole site, resulting in one of the largest hospital developments in Europe. A poignant moment for us and many other local families was the demolition of the old St Mary's building in spring 2010, with its top-floor delivery room, from which I once took a photograph of our house.

Early days in The Groves were taken up with sorting out the house. There were a few conversations with some of the neighbours, but most took little notice of us. Some of the attention we got was not favourable. On one occasion I brought the band's van home and parked it up the street in front of a windowless wall by the corner shop. There was an anonymous note on it next morning detailing what would happen to it if it was still there that night. For our first Halloween (actually several weeks before it, such was their entrepreneurial spirit) several local children called for a donation. We refused to give them anything. Next morning there was paint spilled on our car. A mental note was made for the following year.

Incidents like these made us feel insecure and wonder if we were doing the right thing. But we were also getting to know some of our neighbours and that, together with our sense of calling, kept us going.

Sometimes the negative experiences would result in a positive. One evening we discovered that some glass had been smashed on our car. Nothing had been taken as far as we could tell, and then I realised that whoever had done it had also broken a window on every vehicle parked on that side of our street (on another occasion, every vehicle had a wing mirror kicked off). Sweeping out the tiny bits of broken glass, I thought, 'Do I really want to live in a street where this sort of thing happens?' I took the car to a late-night glass replacement garage and found myself in a queue with a number of my neighbours! That shared experience got me chatting with several people for the first time, and cemented us that bit further into the community.

Children and school

In June 1985 our first child was born. As Judith wheeled Daniel along the street in his pram, our Irish Catholic neighbours would come out and place money under his pillow, one also adding a picture of a saint. This was one of the ways in which Daniel unknowingly helped us to get more known and accepted locally. Another came when he started nursery at the local primary school, just a few minutes' walk away. Judith got to know several of the other mums, and I got chatting with some of the dads, when going to and from the school. Judith became a school governor for a time, and I got involved in helping with some practical matters, such as providing a sound system for the school pantomime, and recording a 'Happy Birthday' backing tape for use in assembly as none of the staff at the time could play it on the piano.

This sort of practical involvement, along with other bits of helping or being helped by our neighbours, arose naturally out of our being there, and we would have been aware of our witness as Christians being in our willingness to help, but at this stage there was no further theological reflection or development of our thinking.

Judith also got to know more local mums through a number of years as part of the church parent and toddler group, continuing through the arrival of our other two children, Alannah in 1989 and Holly in 1992. In 1999 Judith returned to paid work as a classroom assistant at the school. This further built up our links and relationships, and one of the benefits, unforeseen at the time, has been that many of the children she worked with then comprise the local teenagers now: they are still respectful!

We were fortunate in that the local primary was, and is, an excellent school. Looking back, we feel our children benefited from being there, in non-academic ways such as mixing with children from many ethnic and cultural backgrounds – there were about 30 first languages – but also academically doing well enough, with support from home, to progress. Several other families from church also sent their children there, giving them, and us, a mutual support network, though the friendships the children established were far wider than just with those they also saw on Sundays.

We were also fortunate to have a good secondary school option not far away. Again, this was located in the inner city, with a highly committed staff, and children from a wide variety of backgrounds. Would we have made the same decisions had either school been a so-called 'failing school'? Maybe not.

We do recognise our experience of seeing our children educated in inner-city schools (with all three progressing to higher education) may not always be the case for a family of incomers like us in the inner city and so have tried not to use it as a standard for anyone else. Our mentors, the Gooders, for example, just a few years earlier, felt it was right to send their daughters, who had attended the local primary school on Brunswick Estate, to secondary schools outside the area. At one point we did move our youngest to another local school (also very good and about the same distance away in the other direction) during Year 5 as the school was going through a difficult period. With four terms to go before leaving and problems with her class not being dealt with by the headmaster, we felt it was a crucial time for her on several levels, not just academically.

However, even with the availability of good local schools, some families at our church over the years have chosen the approach of their children to school age as the time to move to an area where the schools are 'better'. This would be in terms of academic achievement, an important measure of educational growth to be sure, but not the only one. The usually unspoken implication, for those of us who chose to send our children to the local schools, was that we were not giving them the best chance to succeed. Yet friends who moved to work as missionaries overseas and put their children into the village school were regarded as heroes. We identified with an article written by a church planter on an urban estate who used the local school.

> People (usually Christians) outside the area are horrified to hear that all the children on the church plant will be going to the local schools. The common perception is that since the local people go there, it will be 'rough' and the children will emerge at 16 illiterate! ... It is true that the academic record of the schools in our area is not as good as in the 'nice' parts of the city. However, that is more a reflection on the home life of many of the children, than the school itself. If the children are encouraged to study at home and grow up in a stable, disciplined environment, they can do well no matter what the school is like. Judging from the reactions we have had from some Christians, I am forced to wonder whether they worship God or education. They say they want the best for their children, but it seems

that the best is defined for them by the world not the
Bible, and include a degree and a career.[1]

In a number of ways our children are more bicultural
and bilingual than we are, having absorbed values and
beliefs both from us and from the local area. We came here
as incomers but they did not. We are immigrants, but they
are natives.

Their early friendships reflected the make-up of the area
in that they were a mix of white, Asian and African-
Caribbean, though as they got older so the requests for lifts
to visit friends in suburban areas got more frequent,
reflecting the wider catchment area of secondary school as
they tended to gravitate towards children from similar
social backgrounds to their parents. However, the extra
breadth of experience and relationships growing up and
going to school in a multicultural area is something they
have come to appreciate and seen benefits from. In 2007–
2008 one of our daughters spent a gap year working in
Bangalore in India, and found that her upbringing had
prepared her for settling into the local community and
making friends far better than her two co-workers who
came from suburban towns. Both left for the UK before the
end of their time because of illness, and our daughter
remained on her own and, if anything, made even deeper
friendships, several of them ongoing. She has been back
twice since to visit.

We did, of course, have times when we wondered if our
children would survive in schools with a catchment area
that was very mixed and mostly deprived. There was no
shortage of 'problem' children who could disturb classes
and pick on other children, and we had a few crisis

moments. Should we have done what others had done and send them to schools in 'nicer' areas – usually after moving there first? Was it fair to impose our calling to live here on them too? Our feeling, looking back, is that their growing up here and in local schools – *good* local schools – has given them a richer basis for going through adult life.

Many a priest will say to me, 'I cannot in all conscience visit that deprivation upon my family.' My usual rejoinder is to say, 'Can you not see what cultural deprivation you may be introducing your family to if you live in a monocultural, well-heeled parish where no one has a clue about the issues which others face?' But my impassioned plea is not given much credence.[2]

Who is my neighbour?

Most of our neighbours over the years have been ordinary people that we have got on with well and enjoyed getting to know, a mixture of older, long-term residents, couples or people living alone, and various families. There are also some student houses, but owing to the transient nature of student life there is not a lot of contact. We have also had our share of 'problem' families, joy riding and minibikes, and houses where drug-dealing, domestic violence and prostitution have gone on and various criminal activities have been based.

One household in particular consists of a single mother, with a fondness for alcohol, and four children by several fathers, two of whom now have children of their own. The house acts as a magnet for all sorts of people, with frequent comings and goings and occasional confrontations, arguments and fights, often on the street outside the front door. This has also meant the police tend to go there first if any trouble is reported in the area – not always fairly. It was the meeting point for a number of local young men on the night of the summer 2011 riots in Manchester. They returned later wearing a number of new items of clothing.

We actually get on quite well with the various family members and have helped them out with lifts, pens, scissors and tools on numerous occasions, as well as helping Mum get back into the house several times after a drinking spree when she has lost her key. Several years ago we refused to sign a petition being got up by another resident to persuade the housing association to move them on. Our feeling was that they had been a part of our community for nearly 15 years and that had constrained their behaviour to an extent, which would probably not be the case if they were in another area with more similar households. We have tried to be available and to encourage and prompt towards training and employment, and local youth workers have made some significant interventions. Three of the now grown-up children have (mostly) moved away, and one of the boys is in stable employment. One of the girls is also currently holding down a job with a good company, and is working hard to regain custody of her children.

One neighbour's husband of eight months disappeared the day his citizenship came through. Another had Rottweiler, Alsatian and Pit Bull Terrier dogs in his yard and sometimes offered items like duvets and carpet round the doors.[3] He was also a small-time drug dealer who had his car burnt out after trying to go 'freelance'. Not long after being caught in possession of a local garage's steam cleaner (through the simple process of following a trail of oil drips to the back of his van) he went off to prison and the house was re-let.

A family that lived next door for several years called one Friday to ask if they could borrow £5, promising to repay it the next week. On Tuesday they called and repaid us, only to be back on Friday to ask to borrow £5 again. This became a regular occurrence, and we used to keep the £5 note from Tuesday tucked behind a picture frame near the door ready for Friday.

One of our experiences of joy riders involved being awakened in the early hours by the loud bang of their stolen car colliding with our car. They then crashed into a house around the corner and abandoned the car. A neighbour had just finished his taxi-driving shift and had also heard the noise, so we followed the four occupants in his taxi as they staggered off, using its radio to give directions to a police van. They ended up in a kebab shop where the police apprehended them but, despite evidence and witnesses, no charges were brought. It is perhaps not surprising that there is little interest around here in schemes like Neighbourhood Watch, and that stories circulate of other means of dealing with crime and criminals that do not include the involvement of the police.

For a number of years now, at the end of the fasting period of Ramadan, Judith has baked large amounts of chocolate cake which we have then taken round our Muslim neighbours to wish them a Happy Eid. This has often been reciprocated with edible treats arriving at our door. One Afghan dish in particular has become a firm favourite of ours.

We have been able to help various neighbours in practical ways, such as form-filling, checking English, putting up shelves, pushing a non-starting car, getting shopping for a housebound lady, visiting in hospital. Not long ago I had to bribe a taxi driver to take a young mum and her children to a refuge late one night (a subject for an ethics debate). And neighbours have helped us: keeping a spare key, taking in parcels, painting the outside of our house, loan of clothes to Judith for an Asian ladies-only pre-wedding event, and… pushing a non-starting car! We have been to each other's children's birthday parties and then weddings, and also to baptisms and funerals. Some bricks left over from a building job two doors up are now shoring up a chimney breast in our house that was in danger of collapsing.

Several of us, cheered on by a small crowd of children, recently spent an afternoon cutting down and removing a dead tree from behind one of our houses. While probably not an incident to inform a health and safety officer about, we had a lot of laughs and shared a sense of achievement afterwards. Currently, we are helping an Afghan neighbour who has set up a support group for Afghan women to enable them to get out and away from being stuck in their homes every day. We have been able to help with a publicity banner, form-filling and to secure some funding for set-up and running costs.

On a number of occasions we have worked with our neighbours on particular issues that we were all affected by. These have included street lighting, rubbish collection, fly-tipping, smoke and ash from the hospital's waste disposal chimney, a car-parking issue, turning a piece of waste ground into a community garden and improving the local park (about which more later). But most of the time, with most of our neighbours, it is ordinary life on an ordinary street. In recent years we have found that a great way to welcome a new neighbour is to go and help them understand the complexities of taking the bins out, now that we have four different types and a complex pick-up schedule to juggle. This can be a mysterious thing, particularly for those who do not have English as a first language!

In the early 1990s, with a third child on the way, we wondered about lack of space and had a look at a few bigger houses, all close by, but apart from the not inconsiderable jump in price, we just could not feel at ease with leaving this group of streets. A strong feeling I had had several times before came back to me of being placed here by God, like a chess master carefully positions his pieces, and that our primary calling was to 'be' where we had been located. Any tentative plans were shelved and we began to look instead at doing something with our loft. As a step of faith, as we had no means to pay for the work, we got plans drawn up for a loft conversion. These were passed by the council planning department and would be valid for ten years. Shortly after this, in a scene reminiscent of stories in books about miracles, I came home one night to find an envelope in the hall containing a Banker's Draft for £2,000. I woke Judith up to show her: to this day we do not know where it came from. Over the next few weeks we received more donations, some anonymous, some from existing supporters, until, together with what we did have in the bank, there was enough to create the extra room. Space problem solved without moving an inch and, we felt, another confirmation that we were where God had called us to be and that we were to stay put.

Urban Presence

Having spent the first part of our time in the inner city travelling all over the country, by the late 1980s I was working with another band half-time, mostly in the north-west, and also overseeing Youth for Christ's various ministries and projects in the same region. This included supporting a new project in an inner-city area of North Manchester, called 'Urban Action Manchester' (UAM), and characterised by the workers living incarnationally in the context.

After a shaky first year, as the founders discovered that their youth work theory on the whole just did not work with the young people of Moston and Harpurhey, a new model gradually evolved which involved working with young people where they were, on the streets, rather than trying to bring them into buildings. I took on a role of working with churches to build awareness and understanding of the issues facing young people in deprived parts of the city. This led to an invitation to join the coordinating group of Network, an alliance of evangelical churches and organisations trying to link and liaise in Greater Manchester, much as the Evangelical Alliance does nationally.

Within Network I became one half of a sort of 'urban conscience' for the group, which was otherwise all from suburban churches. The other half was Derek Purnell, who lived in Newton Heath in inner-city North Manchester. We discovered we had a similar vision to work with churches and Christians located in inner-city areas. By now I was mostly working just in the Manchester area, and in 1996 I ended my formal links with YFC and we set up Urban Presence. We wanted to encourage and support those who, like ourselves, were there already, whether individuals, organisations or churches, and also educate and challenge the wider Church concerning the inner city as a 'mission field on our doorsteps'.

We felt that the cumulative effect of the drift to the suburbs, and a loss of the 'where' aspect of Christian service limiting movement in the other direction, had left inner-city areas that could be said to fit the Lausanne definition of an unreached people group, originally formulated for overseas mission: 'A people or people group among which there is no indigenous community of believing Christians with adequate numbers and resources to evangelise the rest of its members without outside (cross-cultural) assistance.'[4]

We encouraged Christians to consider becoming 'bi-vocational workers' in response to 'what is basically a "missionary call" to move to an urban area and live and worship there while continuing in their existing jobs'.[5] This was to address the disparity between where most Christians were located and where most of the population lived. For Manchester we estimated that 75 per cent of the people lived in inner-city areas (including overflow estates), and that 75 per cent of Christians lived in suburban areas. This was a 'best guess' based on observation, census figures and statistics in books such as Joslin's *Urban Harvest*,[6] as no comprehensive research had been done to gather more accurate statistics.[7] We felt this was symptomatic of a lack of awareness and interest from a wider Church that was mostly located and focused elsewhere. There were other indicators. As part of a dialogue with the Evangelical Alliance about the urban context, we undertook two pieces of research. One examined the teaching programme over five years of a major Christian conference and showed that out of 425 seminar titles and programme descriptions, none were directly about the Urban Agenda, and only 17 could possibly have had relevant content.[8] The other surveyed Bible and ministerial training colleges: of those that responded, few had dedicated urban modules or courses, and some others had urban topics within other modules.

One of our first pieces of work was with Urban Action Manchester, setting up a new management group and applying for charitable status. Derek and I both served on the management group as trustees for a number of years and UAM was to expand to three projects. Of these, the M13 Youth Project in my area, which I chaired for several years, is now the only one remaining, the other two having been later subsumed into Eden projects.[9] M13 retains a link with YFC, though while clearly Christian in ethos and working, it is very far from being – and is much more than – an evangelistic outreach project.

Initially we worked exclusively with Christian organisations, churches and projects. Often there would be a degree of partnership with other groups and agencies, but this was valued only as being a means to help finance the Christian partner. It was not until beginning to work with Carisma six years later, and then through reflecting on that experience, that I began to reassess and recognise that others, not necessarily Christian, could share concerns and were working positively in their communities. While also maintaining that Christians have a unique contribution to make in terms of relationship with God, it was arrogant to think we had some sort of monopoly on caring and commitment to help people. In more recent years I have tended to speak more of Urban Presence's work as 'resourcing good news' in the city in a wider sense – whoever was trying to make it.

After a number of years of work taking me all over the country, working with Urban Presence has enabled me to concentrate more on Manchester, and from time to time to include local projects as part of my work portfolio (some of these are described later when I look at 'project-praxis' in detail). Judith, too, since the children all reached school age, has been able to 'work where she lives', first as a classroom assistant at the primary school around the corner, and then as an ESOL[10] and Family Learning teacher in the local area.

Interaction with local culture

As with Lockton Court, a lot of our interaction with neighbours is on the street or doorstep. 'Going for a coffee' or being invited round for a meal happens mostly with Muslim neighbours, and rarely with white working-class ones.

We had a graphic experience of the differences between cultures when we had a meal with neighbours who are Pakistani Muslims, for whom hospitality is very important. A delicious home-made curry was served and, as is the polite thing to do in our culture, we cleaned our plates – only to have them instantly refilled. By the third helping we were unable to finish, and only then were the plates taken away. It was only later we discovered – with much mutual amusement – that the polite way to appreciate food in their culture, and signal you have had enough, is to leave some on the plate.

Invitations from white working-class families tend to be weddings, baptisms or birthday parties. A fiftieth birthday party a few years ago involved the usual food, drinks, chat and music with adults and children mixing. Later on the drinking games started, with the children still present, though not taking part. The acceptance of drunkenness is a part of the culture, though interestingly neither Judith nor I were pressed to join in with this part of the evening. It did mean we were able to drive some guests home later (evidence of a general cultural shift in attitude towards drinking and driving). The contrast with Muslim weddings we have been invited to was stark. In this culture people appear to be able to have just as much of a good time without any alcohol being consumed – something our wider Manchester culture could learn from, as the local authority with the one of the worst alcohol harm levels in England.[11]

I mentioned earlier our children's friendships with other children in the area, and how these tended to change as they got older. It depends how you define friendship, but if it is in terms of mutual invitations to weddings, baptisms, birthday parties, meals, long chats on doorsteps (I can hear one going on downstairs as I type this), sharing confidences, then Judith and I would describe quite a few of our neighbours as good friends. Perhaps not to the degree of closeness we have with some of our church friends with whom we also share a Christian faith, but in a few cases, particularly for Judith, not far behind.[12] Some of these friendships go back virtually to when we arrived here in 1983.

Over the years we have not had many conversations with neighbours that could be regarded as overtly 'spiritual', and most of those have been with Muslim neighbours for whom religion is bound up in everyday life and culture (rather than being one of the two things British people traditionally do not talk about). We have not felt it appropriate to push our beliefs, preferring to try to live as good neighbours with integrity, in agreement with Stuart Murray that, 'Evangelism ... is not the starting point for mission in a plural society.'

> Given the horrendous record of intolerance in Christendom and deep mutual suspicion, the priority is to build relationships of respect and friendship. If these are genuine and involve more than a superficial communication, it is perfectly legitimate to share religious convictions and encourage conversion (in either direction).[13]

In that regard, we are respectful of other people's beliefs – particularly so in the case of our Muslim neighbours – and we have problems with trying to force or manipulate conversations in a particular direction as such tactics seem vaguely dishonest. However, the fact that we are committed Christians is known. One evening a local pastor was coming to our house to meet with me. He was a few minutes late. 'Sorry, I forgot your address, so I knocked at a door and said I was looking for the Christian couple and they said it was number 17.'

The negatives

Moving into the neighbourhood is what incarnational ministry is all about, but should not be undertaken lightly. It's not without personal and family cost – and this does need to be considered.[14]

We have, for the most part, found living in Chorlton-on-Medlock a positive experience. Over the years we have had several burglaries and car break-ins, and incidents where our house or possessions have been damaged or vandalised. When the gun crime issue was at its height there were a number of incidents in or near our area. These included a number of shootings and the arrest of two armed suspects late one night who had taken refuge in our backyard. While these are not pleasant or desirable experiences, they have not disturbed our feeling of being settled here to the point of making us consider moving elsewhere.

Our neighbours for the most part have been responsive and friendly. With a couple of exceptions, those that have had or caused problems have not stayed long. The occupants of one house that turned out to be the base for a drug-dealing operation kept a very low profile, and did not tend to have clients calling (unlike two other houses with low-level dealing), presumably to not draw attention to themselves.

Our children (apart from an occasional wistful comment about how big a friend's or cousin's house was) have, we feel, come through their upbringing in an inner-city context well. I have referred earlier to our daughter's ability to mix and settle in a community in Bangalore, and our son chose to live in an area of Sheffield very similar to where he grew up. We are not aware of any resentments or feelings of being deprived in some way but, if anything, an appreciation for the rich variety of cultures that coexist in this place, and maybe even a touch of pride in the 'street savvy' they all possess.

An indicator of our rootedness here can be seen in an incident from a few years ago when our son was surrounded by a group of young men who wanted to steal his money and phone. Suddenly one of them recognised him as being 'from The Groves', and they immediately left him. One cycled up to him later to apologise![15]

However, I am aware of other incomers with very different stories. These have involved resentment from and conflict with local people, problems with struggling inner-city schools, lack of positive support from friends or church. In some cases this has led to them moving out of the area; in others there have been issues with children growing up resentful of their parents' calling and faith, and their time and energy spent on ministry. In all such cases there are no glib and easy answers when the only 'crime' has been to try to follow a perceived calling from God to go against the flow to the suburbs.

Our biggest negative experience had nothing to do with our decision to settle long term in the inner city. This was the sudden death of our son Daniel at 25 from anaphylaxis in December 2010. It took place in Sheffield where he had moved some years previously to study and then met and married Tess and settled. It was a massive shock on all levels, raising many emotions, doubts and questions. We had – and still have – tremendous support from family and friends, particularly from our church, but there was also an outpouring of sympathy and comfort from many of our neighbours, some of whom would have known Daniel growing up on The Groves. They came to talk and listen, they cried with us in our front room and on the street, and a few – including some Muslims – travelled over to Sheffield in hazardous, freezing weather to attend the funeral. Looking back, this tragic experience revealed the depth of acceptance and relationship we have acquired over the many years we have lived here. The trust that we have in some of our neighbours meant that it did not occur to us to hide or minimise our vulnerability as grieving parents, or the struggles we have had with our faith, and though such an outcome could not have been further from our minds at the time, this openness has led to these relationships being deepened further.

---

[1] Steve Wood, 'When The Going Gets Tough,' *New Christian Herald*, 20th July 1996.
[2] Laurie Green, 'I Can't Go *There!*', in Andrew Davey, ed. *Crossover City* (London: Mowbray, 2010) p.2.

3 These would have 'fallen off the back of a lorry' – ie were stolen goods.

4 Lausanne Committee Strategy Working Group, Chicago, 16th March 1982.

5 http://www.urbanpresence.org.uk/services.html (accessed 4th October 2016). This could be described as a 'where' vocation paired with a 'what' vocation.

6 Roy Joslin, *Urban Harvest: Biblical perspectives on Christian Mission in the inner cities* (Welwyn: Evangelical Press, 1982).

7 Confirmed by Peter Brierley, director of Christian Research in correspondence with Derek Purnell in 2000.

8 Paul Keeble, *A Survey of Spring Harvest Programme Seminar Information, 1996–2000* (Manchester: Urban Presence, 2001).

9 Eden is a network of youth and community projects located in deprived neighbourhoods. More in part four.

10 English for Speakers of Other Languages.

11 Public Health England, *Local Alcohol Profiles for England*, June 2015. I have been involved with Street Pastors since it started in Manchester in 2004 and have seen the damage caused by our drinking culture close up.

12 One of her closest friends is a Muslim neighbour, and for some years now Judith has been a part of a larger group of Asian women who have occasional evenings out.

13 Stuart Murray, *Post-Christendom: Church and Mission in a Strange New World* (Carlisle: Paternoster, 2004) p.234.

14 Eleanor Williams, top ten tips for starting an urban fresh expression. Moving into the area is her number two, number one being to have a clear sense of call. 'Urban fresh expressions', Fresh Expressions. http://www.freshexpressions.org.uk/guide/examples/urban (accessed 5th October 2016).

15 Ardwick has a number of student residences and houses, and the mugging rate is among the highest in Manchester.

http://menmedia.co.uk/manchestereveningnews/news/s/1490377_crime-down-your-street-robbery-hotspot-in-the-heart-of-manchester (accessed 5th October 2016).

Becoming and being one of the neighbours: reflections on 'presence-among'

In our case the practice of 'mission-with' has involved relocating to a culturally different area as incomers. In this section I want to draw attention to the significance of living ordinary life to the 'mission-with' model, and then look at the implications of seeking to be a 'presence-among' under the headings, Whose culture?, Bringing God or Finding God?, and Whose church?

Mission as normal life

We have long felt very comfortable living where we do and now feel to a large degree accepted as 'locals'. While this is largely because of the length of time we have been here and factors such as sending our children to local schools, I think it can also be attributed to the fact that we have seen this area in a very straightforward way as being just 'where we live'.

Most of the time we are living ordinary life doing the sorts of things neighbours do everywhere. The important differences are that we are doing it with an awareness of missional implications, we are doing it here – having considered the 'where' as well as the 'what' – and we are not following the aspirational pattern of many of our middle-class peers. The significance of the incarnational notions of identification and being sent for 'presence-among' will be discussed later. Suffice to say here that for 'mission-with' it means discovering the 'with whom', and therefore the 'where', are as important in finding and following our calling as the 'what'. Being a 'presence among' can and should be a part of a Christian's life in any community, inner city, suburban or rural, but taking the 'where' of calling seriously should lead to a significant degree of redressing of the imbalance of where Christians tend to live.

Can a Christian's 'mission' be equivalent to, or at least based on, one's normal life lived with an awareness of oneself as a Christian (a 'whole-life faith' as opposed to a dualistic 'add-on devotional to ... suburban, professional life'[1])? It may include some intentionality and some praxis which is more overt, but the basis is a life lived in a house in a street in a local area in a city, alongside other people; a life *which can be observed*. This has been the experience of other Christian incomers.

> Our lives are watched and our faith is seen being put into practice. It's the same model Jesus used. People can judge for themselves whether it makes a genuine difference but our hope and our prayer is that our presence in this community will bring about lasting and positive change in people's lives.[2]

This is not meant to be a heavy expectation, but an awareness of the fact that all people, through their everyday actions and choices, reveal something of their world views and values in subtle or obvious ways. If I am known as a Christian, then that will impinge on all my interactions with my neighbours. So when, in a re-enactment of one of Jesus' stories, one of them rang the doorbell at just before midnight asking if I could phone for a taxi for her as her phone was out of credit, my response would have been logged and her evaluation of my Christian faith slightly adjusted accordingly, even if subconsciously. And again, when the same request was made a few weeks later.

As the first ingredient of 'working for the *shalom* of your city', Linthicum draws a parallel to the instruction in Jeremiah 29:5-7 to the Jewish exiles in Babylon to 'seek the welfare of the city' (ESV) through the ordinary elements of life. 'Welfare' here is the Hebrew *shalom*. Linthicum paraphrases the passage:

> Don't isolate yourself from the rest of the Babylonian community and create a Jewish ghetto. Enter fully into the life of that city. Get a job and enter into its economy. Buy a house or rent an apartment. Become a Yahweh-lover who loves your city's people and commits himself or herself to its life and being. Weep with those who weep. Laugh with those who laugh. Live and move and have your being in the city as people who are transformed by the magnetic love of Jesus Christ. And by so doing, become God's presence in the city to which I have called you.[3]

This adds a depth to living among and with, by placing a significance on the normal. God places as much value in the everyday actions of believers living among and being observed by others as people of faith as He does in a special evangelistic event. But does the Church? Rather than 'this is the mission field to which I feel called to lay down my life in service' with its heroic overtones, it is simply, 'this is where I live'. How effective or authentic is mission praxis which one travels elsewhere to do, where daily integrity is not really a factor? That sort of episodic praxis may feel more like real mission activity and therefore more appealing but, though requiring effort and commitment, could be said to be actually *less* costly than one where there is no 'On Duty' sign and no 'Off' switch.

We have been asked on a number of occasions by Christian friends if we see ourselves being here for the rest of our lives. The answer again relates to our calling: our default is to stay, unless and until we feel God is calling us elsewhere (and it is important that we stay open to all possibilities). Again, the 'where' is as important as the 'what' – maybe more so. This is home, and will continue to be, but of course never say never in the kingdom of God. Just look at Abraham!

Another question we have been asked is whether we have ever felt a sense of ingratitude ('Don't these people realise we've come to help? Don't they know what we've given up?'). This question is rooted in a misunderstanding of why we are in this place. We did not come here to help people. We came here to live, to be residents and neighbours, to get to know and be known by our fellow residents, to love our neighbours as ourselves. We see ourselves as equals, not some sort of rescuing angels. We are here as much to learn from and be helped by our neighbours as to help and encourage them. One of the things we bring with us, which we hope influences our attitudes and behaviour, is our relationship with Jesus.

As for what we have given up, we honestly struggle to name anything significant. We didn't move here from a detached house with a big garden and a lovely view, so that isn't something we miss or have a particular aspiration to acquire. We have deliberately not fully exploited our earning potential to free up time for being with people, but as loving both God and money is not possible according to Matthew 6:24, surely that is something all Christians should weigh up and recheck from time to time.

Whose culture?

I have described some of the ways in which we have interacted with our neighbours and ways in which we have sought to learn from and adapt to their cultures. But of course we bring a culture with us. As incomers and guests of a host culture, what do we need to consider and how should we behave as we interact and relate? I have found the notions of a continuum and becoming 'bicultural' helpful as ways to understand this dynamic. Again, the importance of the ordinary is clear.

Tamara Kohn in her study of a remote Scottish island describes an 'incomer/islander continuum' – a line along which incoming non-islanders would move, or not, as members of the population. Kohn asserts that the way to progress along the continuum was not by self-conscious adoption or manipulation of symbols of the culture but through engaging in 'that "action" that takes place in the humdrum of everyday life' and that this may be a 'more revealing marker of identity'.[4] The processes of becoming part of a community can be:

> very quietly and subtly enacted and embodied by people in the everyday. In fact, they might be so quiet and subtle as to be invisible to the very people that they define.[5]

The concept of a continuum is helpful as it implies movement towards and an ongoing and living process. This was largely the case for us and something we came to realise with hindsight rather than being part of a deliberate strategy. Of course that realisation could lead to it becoming an ongoing strategy, which could in turn nudge our praxis towards the self-conscious.

There is a balance to be found here between two extremes. One is a deliberate and self-conscious adopting of local ways and symbols as a means to gaining acceptance so that the gospel can be shared. The other is living normally and gradually absorbing these ways and symbols, but without any sense of self-awareness as a Christian – maybe through a sense of duality where 'Christian' is a mode for certain times and places. Trying to find a balance means that most of the time you are erring on one side or the other, if only slightly. Being aware of the dynamic, but not in any intense way, can help to be an ongoing corrective. This is, after all, about ordinary life, so getting on with it is the best way to proceed.

> For those who do want to 'belong', it is through action that we see them adopting new ways of being and doing – sometimes highly self-consciously, and

yet often unself-consciously and unreflexively, but always meaningfully.[6]

Given this continuum from outsider to insider that the incomer moves along as differing cultures meet, how and to what degree differing cultures adapt, are altered, or mix when they come together has led to various models being put forward for how cultural identity is acquired. In the area of bicultural competence, alternation is an additive model describing how a second culture can be known and understood. It is then possible to 'alternate' between the two, to adopt behaviour that fits in with a particular social situation. Our children's ability to switch into a broader Mancunian 'street' accent and vocabulary when with other local children is a clear example of this altering of behaviour to fit context. This adapting to fit in is not something we deliberately taught them to do, though we may well have modelled it to some extent.[7]

The capacity to become bicultural and its possible extent is explored by Malcolm McFee in his study of Blackfoot Indians acculturation into white American society. He suggests a concept where individuals are able to take on up to 75 per cent of the other culture, but also retaining 75 per cent of their own – in effect being '150% men'.[8] McFee also speaks of 'Interpreters', certain Indians in the bicultural milieu who learn to mediate between the two cultures and how they relate.

> The Interpreters can talk to and better understand both sides. Yet they are Indian-oriented. They live with and want to be accepted by the Indian group and to maintain their Indian identity.[9]

This parallels the experience of several individuals I know from inner-city working-class culture who have become Christians and learned some of the middle-class culture of the Church, but stayed true to their roots. They have a unique role in mission in aiding cross-cultural communication and mutual understanding which should be valued much more.

Adopting McFee's 150 per cent concept, Lingenfelter and Mayers use an incarnational model of a cross-cultural missioner, following the example of Jesus who was the only true fully bicultural '200-percent person, fully God and fully human in the life and world of Jewish culture'.[10] Though writing primarily out of overseas missionary experience, their observations apply equally well to working-class and middle-class cultural differences, some of which I have referred to, such as books or videos, holiday destinations, having coffee, different meanings for 'dinner' and 'tea'.[11]

Given 200 per cent is impossible:

> we must be willing to become 150-percent persons. We must accept the value priorities of others. We must learn the definitions and rules of the context in which they live. We must adopt their patterns and procedures for working, playing and worshipping. We must become incarnate in their culture and make them our family and friends.[12]

I would suggest that the 50 per cent overlap is an inevitable tension that must be lived with, along with a feeling of not being entirely 'at home' in either culture as 'there will be stress involved in the process of acquiring competence in a second culture while maintaining affiliation with one's culture of origin'.[13] Accepting the values of others and adopting their patterns needs to be done critically and there will be frictions and dilemmas. This must be balanced by placing our own values and patterns under similar scrutiny, especially where they could cause misunderstanding or offence. Lingenfelter and Mayers elsewhere qualify their advocacy for missionaries wholly entering into the culture of those they are among by adding, 'Moreover, they must do this in the spirit of Christ, that is, without sin.'[14] Paul's wisdom in deciding which issues to concede and on which to make a stand, and when – such as food offered to idols, circumcision, eating with Gentiles – is an example of engaging with different cultures while retaining integrity with his Christian beliefs.[15]

So, to return to an earlier consideration of cost and what we have given up, perhaps it is bound up in that 50 per cent overlap where the culture we have come from and the culture we have come into clash and contradict each other. An example would be not fitting in with the drinking culture at that fiftieth birthday party. But one of the many remarkable things about our neighbours is that they recognised and were sensitive to our possible discomfort and there were no problems.

Bringing God or finding God?

Given the missional aspect of our decision to live in this community in response to a sense of calling from God, in what sense, if any, does the missioner bring God into a context? Or was God at work in the context before the missioner got there? If the mission of the Church is seen as a part of the complete mission of God – the *missio Dei* – then God has always been active in His world, and continues to be, independently of, as well as through, the missional work of the Church.

So, what role does the Church have to play? Is it dispensable? In one sense it is. God can always find other ways to achieve His purposes. But, historically, God has chosen to use people to reach people with the message of His love for us and desire for relationship with us. This is a theme of the Old Testament with His choice of the people of Israel, and is shown supremely in the coming of Jesus who told of and showed the Father, and began to train a group of His followers to continue His mission of bringing this good news to the world. With further training promised through the coming of the Holy Spirit, Jesus commissioned this group to continue His work. 'This is the message we have heard from him and declare to you …'[16]

In considering in what sense God is mediated by the incoming missioner, there are two extremes to be avoided. One is to think that the missioner brings God with them into the context, which is to say that previously God was somehow absent. The other is to suppose that, in our culture and long history of Christian teaching and influence, any particular context is already sufficiently exposed to God and the missioner is therefore only a reinforcer of what is already present – all are already children of God. While there may be situations that approach either extreme, it would be unlikely that any were totally ignorant or cognisant in knowledge of the gospel and commitment to God. The answer would appear to be somewhere between the extremes:

> We can always be challenged by and learn from those who are suffering, but if we bring nothing we have no mission. Although Christ is already present in the city, this is rarely perceived; while we may debate whether we bring Christ, we certainly should reveal him.[17]

Donovan puts it this way: 'He [God] was there before we ever got there. It is simply up to us to bring him out so they can recognise him.'[18]

There is a significant place for the missioner, and something they can add, but there is also a need to first find out where the local people are up to – which will be somewhere beyond square one – and respectfully begin there.

Ann Morisy states that Christians have something worth sharing in social action which is neither an unconditional gift – ie devoid of gospel content – nor a pretext for evangelism, or indeed taking advantage of the vulnerable. If we have experienced faith in Jesus as having made a difference to us, and we believe it could be beneficial to the well-being of another and their community, then to 'respond only to people's social welfare needs, when this Christian faith is assessed in having played a profound role in one's own well-being, is oddly inconsistent'.[19]

In a discussion about communicating the gospel to others, Tillich speaks of the importance of identifying with people, but not to the point of losing our distinctiveness:

> We can speak to people only if we participate in their
> concern, not by condescension, but by sharing in it.
> We can point to the Christian answer only if, on the
> other hand, we are not identical with them.[20]

The addition of a fresh perspective could help local people long immersed in the context. Vincent notes that 'the problem often is the absence of people who can get a proper perspective on the local situation, sufficient to be able to see ways of development and change'. And that 'a bit of distance, as in objectivity, can be a good thing, complementing the close-up, seeing the wood for the trees, bringing new perspectives, so long as it serves and does not assume control'.[21] However, he goes on to emphasise that this must be from a basis of being with, hence sharing in the issues and experience of the context:

> The real contrast is not with people who come in,
> and those who are there already. The real contrast is
> between locals and incomers on the one side, and the
> permanent outsiders – those who presume to
> evaluate or dictate what is to be done, who never
> become incomers, but remain outsiders, be it as
> professionals or critics.[22]

In a number of passages in Acts there is evidence of awareness of God, if not of response to and worship of God, before the arrival of the missioner.[23] However, the missioner brought fresh insight and revelation to do with the person and work of Jesus that built upon what they already knew and took them to a new place of commitment and relationship. So Philip begins with the passage in

Isaiah the Ethiopian official was reading, and Paul in Athens, seeing that they are 'very religious', begins by speaking about the inscription on one of their altars: 'You worship a god that you don't know, and this is the God I am telling you about!'[24]

It is also clear, however, especially from Acts 10, that the revelation was not all one-way. Through his encounter with Cornelius, Peter is significantly moved forward in his understanding of God and in the universality of the gospel.

'Presence-among' is with a missional intent, balanced by a recognition that the missioner is there as a learner and as one who finds God there already ahead of them. Any genuine relationship changes both parties and is an end in itself, not a means to 'making them like me' or even sharing the gospel in an overt way. Laurie Green speaks of entering in 'with trepidation ... as we are on "holy ground"'. 'The purpose of our entering into the marginal place is not to impose our culture or to win spiritual "market share" but to give ourselves away, to listen with rapt attention and to meet Jesus there.'[25]

While not hiding the fact of being a church-goer or having Christian faith, any sharing of that faith is primarily through actions and attitudes and getting to know and be known by people through building relationships and friendships. It is, therefore, initially mostly non-verbal – in contrast to engineering 'opportunities' for conversations about faith, something regarded as good practice in some evangelical circles. Incomer Sara Jane Walker speaks of having to constantly let go of her agendas and 'show up as I am – with humility', ready to 'participate in the common good as it is named by my neighbours':

Joining God at work in my neighbourhood is not a back entry or a secret path to converting my neighbours. It is not an evangelisation tactic. It is a reorientation of what it means to follow Jesus. It takes me out of my place of power and control (performing actions and activities to move people from point 'a' to 'b') to being a participant in the work of the Spirit.[26]

Instead, any verbal sharing of faith is by responding to questions asked or remarks made by others. Particularly in the initial period of settling in and beginning and building relationships, we felt there was a need for a kind of 'intentional passivity', being responsive rather than proactive, not necessarily taking the initiative, asking for help and letting people give us advice and do things for us.[27] After all, they had the local knowledge. This was a way of getting on with, 'If it is possible, as far as it depends on you, live at peace with everyone.'[28]

It may be helpful, particularly for evangelicals, to remember that both the Great Command and the New Command precede the Great Commission and should be the lens through which we implement it.[29] Seeing the Great Commission in this way, without devaluing it, is picked up in an article by Cindy Brandt in which she turns the notion of evanglising on its head.

The biggest problem I have with evangelizing is that you enter into a relationship with a prescribed intention, and that stands in the way of listening well. You can't listen well when you are carrying an agenda. You can't listen well when you are looking for ways to fortify your own position. You can't listen well when you are searching for what is broken in your conversation partner, in order to introduce the solution. ... We earn our right to speak into other people's lives when we have logged enough hours listening to their truths, and been willing to be changed by their beauty. We compel people to join our cause and believe in our God when we thread the Great Commandment into the Great Commission: love your neighbor as yourself.[30]

Philip Yancey comments, 'It makes all the difference in the world whether I view my neighbour as a potential convert or as someone who God already loves.'[31]

Though 'love your neighbour as yourself' is listed as the second of the Great Commandments that Jesus gave, it is described as 'like' the first, the Greek word meaning 'the same as'. For those who remember the old vinyl 45rpm single records, the two commandments are like a Double A-Side. Could it be that loving our neighbour and loving God are equivalents and each expressive of the other? And let us not forget the most obvious meaning of 'neighbour', for which the Greek word also means, simply, 'near'.

Whose church?

An interesting variation on 'whose culture' is one invariable consequence of mission that historically has had to be imported. This is the governance and running of the Church, particularly when predetermined models are required.

In Brunswick, Martin Gooder accepted membership and commitment from several individuals and families who were based further away and did not decide to move in, and indeed he credits their input (especially in the early days of building up the church) as being crucial. The understanding and basis was that the main focus was on the local parish area and their role one of supporting and resourcing local ministry and locally based believers. The aim was to build a congregation of locally based Christians, combining local people and incomers. 'Commuters are not encouraged, but those from outside wanting to settle in the area are.'[32] But it was the commuters and those of us who had moved in who seemed to graduate towards the PCC and leading services, fellowship groups and meetings.

The dependence on imported leadership was attributed to a dearth of suitable skills in the local community. Gooder notes that the people with ability and aspiration tended to be those who could, and therefore did, move away. A big surge in this exodus occurred when compensation funds were made available during the redevelopment of the area, leaving behind those who 'did not have the money, ability or initiative to get out'.[33] This did not just affect the church; attempts to establish tenants' associations failed, and local schools had great difficulty in recruiting parent governors.

> So the church starts a long way back in terms of growing indigenous leadership in that kind of community, and I do not believe the 'doctrine' that all we have to do is find the natural leaders – in 20 years I've met very few.[34]

But could another issue be having to organise the local church according to denominational requirements? Gooder regarded the Church of England as an awkward fit with inner-city working-class culture, but was the 'leadership' required equated with ability to lead and teach in a certain Anglican way? *The Brunswick Papers* includes a paper written by a curate, 'The Nature of an Inner-City Congregation', which says that a church where 'most or all the members come from a relatively socially and educationally deprived class is a church that will fail in many basic Christian functions, notably teaching and leadership'.[35]

Notwithstanding the nature of the community, this begs the question of what measure of teaching and leadership is being used here, and raises the issue of the effect of middle-class and institutional culture, aspiration and method being mixed in with the gospel values being taught and therefore, perhaps inadvertently, being a causal factor in Christians leaving the inner city.

Laurie Green calls the urban a 'difficult environment for the more traditional church':

> For while such a church expects its members to engage in rather antiquated forms of committee decision-making, to assume a dominantly middle-class, literate culture and commit free time weekly on a regular basis, the urban scene simply does not function in that way.[36]

He expands the cultural mismatch to 'forms of interaction and worship which do not come easy to local people',[37] but does not blame the local people for the problem.

Hudson Taylor's revolution of the missionary methods of his time was a reaction to Christianity being perceived as a foreign religion, taking converts out of their native culture:

> It is not their denationalization but their Christianization that we seek. We wish to see Christian (Chinese) – true Christians, but withal true Chinese in every sense of the word.[38]

Writing from an African context, Donovan contends that the Western European culture-bound concept of Church is not part of the gospel. The local culture should be allowed to shape churches and worship, risky though that may be, and in his case a source of tension with the sending body. He challenges assumptions of cultural superiority:

> Are Masai pagans further away from salvation than European and American? Is endemic and incurable cattle thieving further removed from salvation than assassinating and killing and selling deadly weapons and cheating in business and lying in advertising?[39]

Is mission in inner-city areas unnecessarily hobbled by having to use culturally unsuitable models? Is it a price that has to be paid to be part of a bigger, supporting, 'sending' institution? Hasler writes of a 'suburbo-centric' Church 'dominated by managerial and professional thinking'[40] which is incompatible with non-suburban, white middle-class contexts, and appeals for research into 'ways to respond to what is sociologically coherent on the ground'.[41]

Pioneers such as Hudson Taylor and Vincent Donovan – who attempted to bring to the Chinese and Masai people a gospel message unencumbered by centuries of Western European culture[42] – and their modern equivalents[43] took huge risks, not least of isolation, and were much misunderstood and criticised. Would a simpler definition of Church serve such communities better? Donovan believed that once God's love and its demonstration in Christ had been explained, the missioner's job is complete as he had 'come to the end of the good news'.[44] His job is to preach 'not the church, but Christ' and 'any valid, positive response to the Christian message could and should be recognized and accepted as church'.[45]

Donovan was in a very different context and culture, and it could be argued that some continuity and interface with the wider historical Church forms and functions should be ensured, but the same principle of flexibility to allow for culturally relevant expression of Church surely applies.

Probably the ideal to aim for would be a balance between support, accountability and an appreciation of being a part of a continuing history on the one hand, and local autonomy with freedom to develop in ways sensitive to the local culture on the other, while seeking to utilise the complementary strengths of both.

What would a '150 per cent' bicultural church look like?

Results

What about 'results'? Have I 'failed' because I have not done my incoming as 'hi-viz Christianity',[46] being a lot more overt about verbally sharing my faith, and am unable to point to many converts? It partly depends on what counts as 'fruit', which is related to one's definition of mission. Those who see mission more narrowly in only spiritual terms with activities and projects will tend to speak in terms of sowing the gospel (usually verbally) and reaping converts. Biblical terms to be sure, but not that far removed from 'investment and return' and in danger of being influenced by our modern capitalist society's results-driven culture. This can lead to a tendency to serve 'only on the basis of there being "fruit", evidences of my service making a difference'[47] – ie only where, or in ways which generate certain acceptable kinds of result. If it isn't 'working', move on – perhaps to somewhere less 'difficult'. Paul speaks of his planting seed, which is watered by another, but it is God who gives the growth: three clear job descriptions![48] As Mark Greene points out, 'there is no evidence that evangelists receive a greater reward than those who ploughed the ground or those who sowed the seed.'[49]

Greene gives 'fruit' a wide definition as 'anything that brings glory to God', including 'any attitude, any word, any action that pleases God' and 'any consequence that is in line with his will – an animal properly cared for, a local pond cleaned up, a person saved, healed, fed, given a cup of water, taught, corrected, trained in righteousness, defended, rescued from injustice or loved in any godly way. Fruit is anything done with authentic love'.[50] So, not just conversions, then, and I would add inspiring or encouraging others to acts of caring and unselfishness – ie things from the above list that count as creating *shalom*. (I would further add recognising and praising such actions when they occur *without* any input from me: we Christians do not have a monopoly on doing good.)

Of course, part of me would love to be able to list and impress with overtly spiritual results, but for every Jonah who gets to see revival in the city he is sent to, there is at least one Jeremiah who ministers faithfully but with no obvious success of that sort.[51] As Christians are we called to be obedient or successful (however that is to be defined).

We often feel powerless and frustrated at the persistence of an underconfident mindset in some of our neighbours that limits their aspirations and keeps their world small: a variation on 'better the devil you know'. There have been days when I have wondered, when looking at another load of fly-tipping during the night before, if we have been wasting our time here. But unlike the commercial world, our remaining here is not contingent on seeing a return on our investment or a need to 'cut our losses'. Our relationships with our neighbours are not conditional on their responding to the gospel according to some sort of evangelical formula. Anyway, if God's love for us (and them) is unconditional, surely ours is to mirror that. What I keep coming back to is the essence of our calling to *be* in this place, as ordinary residents and neighbours, and of course as Christians. Everything should flow from that, and it is up to God to give the growth.

Philip Yancey quotes Henri Nouwen's description of a mission trip where he set out to educate the 'poor and unenlightened'. During his stay he discovered that:

> a desire to save, whether from sin, poverty or exploitation, is one of the most damaging motives in ministry. 'Humility is the real Christian virtue,' says Nouwen. 'When we come to realise that … only God saves, then we are free to serve, then we can live truly humble lives.' Nouwen changed his approach from 'selling pearls', or peddling the good news, to 'hunting for the treasure' already present in those he was called to love – a shift from dispensing religion to dispensing grace.[52]

Something we have been able to do is help our Muslim neighbours to learn that there is a difference between 'christian' in a social or cultural sense, where a relationship with God is shallow or nonexistent, and 'Christian' in a committed sense of being someone who is trying to follow Jesus. This is an important early step for people of another faith (who may have been taught that everyone in England was a Christian) in coming to understand and appreciate real faith in Jesus. Will those seeds be watered and will God give growth? As with all of our neighbours, that is our hope and prayer. We haven't finished here yet.

---

[1] Tom Sine quoted in Janet I. Tu, 'Christian communities try "whole-life faith"', *Seattle Times*, 29th July 2006.
http://community.seattletimes.nwsource.com/archive/?date=200 60429&slug=church29m (accessed 5th October 2016).

[2] Interview with Rich and Emma Newby, Hull YFC, *Youth for Christ News*, Autumn/Winter 2012.

[3] Linthicum, *Building a People of Power*, p.92. 'Magnetic' echoes Kreider's 'fascination' which will be discussed later.

[4] Tamara Kohn, 'Becoming an Islander through Action in the Scottish Hebrides', *The Journal of the Royal Anthropological Institute*, Vol. 8, no. 1, 2002, p.145.

[5] Kohn, 'Becoming an Islander', p.145.

[6] Kohn, 'Becoming an Islander', p.150.

[7] 'The alternation model of second-culture acquisition assumes that it is possible for an individual to know and understand two different cultures. It also supposes that an individual can alter his or her behaviour to fit a particular social context. ... [it] suggests that it is possible to maintain a positive relationship with both cultures without having to choose between them. ... this model does not assume a hierarchical relationship between two cultures. Within this framework, it is quite possible for the individual to assign equal status to the two cultures, even if he or she does not value or prefer them equally. ... The more an individual is able to maintain an active and effective relationship through alternation between both cultures, the less difficulty he or she will have in acquiring and maintaining competency in both cultures.' Teresa LaFramboise, Hardin L. Coleman, Jennifer Gerton, 'Psychological Impact of Biculturalism: Evidence and Theory', *Psychological Bulletin*, Vol. 114, no. 3, 1993, pp.399–400, p.402.

[8] Malcolm McFee, 'The 150% Man: A Product of Blackfeet Acculturation', *American Anthropologist* 70, 1968, pp.1096–1107.

[9] McFee, 'The 150% Man', p.1100.

[10] Sherwood G. Lingenfelter and Marvin K. Mayers, *Ministering Cross-Culturally*, 2nd edn (Grand Rapids, MI: Baker, 2003) p.122.

[11] 'We had our dinner at what you would call lunchtime and tea was a meal as well as a drink. We were never invited out to supper but in the vanishingly unlikely event that we had been,

my parents would have expected a cup of cocoa and a biscuit.'
Philip Collins, 'Schools are not the way out of the middle-class',
The Times, 9th September 2010.

[12] Lingenfelter and Mayers, *Ministering Cross-Culturally*, p.122.
[13] LaFramboise et al., 'Psychological Impact of Biculturalism',
p.408.
[14] Lingenfelter and Mayers, *Ministering Cross-Culturally*, p.23.
[15] 1 Corinthians 8:4ff & 10:23ff; Acts 16:1-3 (cf. Galatians 2:3);
Galatians 2:11ff.
[16] 1 John 1:5.
[17] Derek Purnell, 'Faith Sharing', in Eastman and Latham, eds.,
Urban Church, p.127.
[18] Vincent Donovan, *Christianity Rediscovered*, 3rd edn (London:
SCM, 2001) p.47.
[19] Ann Morisy, *Beyond The Good Samaritan: Community Ministry
and Mission* (London: Continuum, 1997) p.6.
[20] Paul Tillich, *Theology of Culture* (Oxford: University Press,
1959) p.207.
[21] Vincent, *Hope from the City*, p.126.
[22] Vincent, *Hope from the City*, p.126.
[23] Acts 8:26ff: Philip and the Ethiopian official; 10:1ff: Peter and
Cornelius; 17:16ff: Paul in Athens; 19:1ff: disciples of John.
[24] Acts 17:22-23 (NCV).
[25] Green, 'I Can't Go *There!*', p.5.
[26] Sara Jane Walker, 'Walking the Children to School: A
Neighbourhood Story', *Journal of Missional Practice*, Spring 2016,
http://journalofmissionalpractice.com/author/sara-jane-walker
(accessed 5th October 2016).
[27] Something more activist churches may struggle with: 'Church
life rewards us for being self-starters, group leaders and those
that make things happen.' Walker, 'Walking the Children to
School'.
[28] Romans 12:18.

[29] Matthew 22:37-39; John 13:34: Matthew 28:18-20. 'To my questioner who asks "How do you bring the Gospel into this work?" I answer: begin with the fundamentals. The great command and the new command will take you where you need to go. As St. Francis of Assisi said, "Preach the gospel and use words when necessary."' Robert Lupton, 'Evangelism is More Than Words', *Urban Perspectives* (Atlanta: FCS Urban Ministries, July 2012), http://www.fcsministries.org/fcs-ministries/blog/evangelism-is-more-than-words (accessed 5th October 2016).

[30] Cindy Brandt, *How I Kissed Evangelizing Goodbye* (11th August 2014), http://cindywords.com/how-i-kissed-evangelism-goodbye (accessed 11th October 2016).

[31] Philip Yancey, *Vanishing Grace: Whatever Happened to the Good News?* (London: Hodder & Stoughton, 2015) p.31.

[32] Gooder, *Brunswick Papers*, p.31.

[33] Gooder, *Brunswick Papers*, p.19.

[34] Gooder, *Brunswick Papers*, p.19.

[35] Gooder, *Brunswick Papers*, p.30.

[36] Green, 'I Can't Go *There*!', p.3.

[37] Green, 'I Can't Go *There*!', p.3.

[38] Hudson Taylor, *China's Spiritual Needs and Claims*, 3rd edn (1868), appendix. Quoted in Marshall Broomhall, *The Jubilee Story of the China Inland Mission* (London: Marshall & Scott, 1915) p.32.

[39] Donovan, *Christianity Rediscovered*, p.45.

[40] Joe Hasler, *Crying out for a Polycentric Church: Christ centred and culturally focused congregations* (Maidstone: Church in Society, 2006) p.106.

[41] Hasler, *Crying out for a Polycentric Church*, p.107.

[42] Donovan's model for taking the gospel to a geographically foreign culture has been studied in Emerging Church and Fresh Expressions as a template for mission to postmodern and post-Christian cultures seen as socially foreign. For example:

http://www.missionaloutreachnetwork.com/profiles/blogs/a-reflective-review-of (accessed 5th October 2016).

[43] Living Stones is a contemporary example of church planting as missional community in an urban culture with a deliberate avoidance of any conscious adopting of an off-the-peg imported model, http://www.livingstonesnewtonheath.org.uk (accessed 5th October 2016).

[44] Donovan, *Christianity Rediscovered*, p.66.

[45] 'Institutionalized and structured in a way entirely different from ours, or noninstitutionalized, nonstructured and nonorganized, this response of theirs, as strange as it might seem to us, must be recognized as the church, or we are doing violence to Christianity.' Donovan, *Christianity Rediscovered*, pp.66, 68.

[46] 'Hi-Viz Christianity means that the church of Jesus has deliberately and noticeably positioned itself back into those places from which it had withdrawn.' Matt Wilson, *Eden: Called to the Streets* (Kingsway: London, 2005) p.88.

[47] From a reflection on the writings of W. H. Vanstone who takes a wider and deeper view: 'Vanstone serves to counter my tendency to serve only on the basis of there being "fruit," evidences of my service making a difference. This is the Jesus-way. The quiet way of faithfulness. This is what Vanstone would call the 'deep end' of life, church, and mission. Vanstone encourages me in the slow and lonely work of imagining something different; of seeing this place and the missio Dei within it, differently. Vanstone encourages me to persevere, to trust God; for this is God's work.' Paul Fromont, 'Rev. W. H. Vanstone in the Suburbs,' Prodigal Kiwi(s) Blog, http://prodigal.typepad.com/prodigal_kiwi/2005/11/rev_w_h_v anston.html> (accessed 5th October 2016).

[48] 1 Corinthians 3:6: 'I planted the seed, Apollos watered it, but God has been making it grow.'

[49] Mark Greene, *Fruitfulness on the Frontline: Making a difference where you are* (Nottingham: Inter-Varsity Press, 2014) p.35.

[50] Greene, *Fruitfulness on the Frontline*, p.35.

[51] Jeremiah 7:26: 'But they did not listen to me or pay attention.'

[52] Yancey, *Vanishing Grace*, p.31.

Part Three

What – Projects: Story and Reflection

True incarnation is when I go out and get involved in a local project where I don't run the show and I don't pull all the strings.[1]

[1] Steve Chalke. Quote from 'Faith in Politics', Christian Socialist Movement Conference 2001.

Up to now I have concentrated, with a few diversions, on how I came to live in an inner-city area of Ardwick, Manchester and on life in that community. If you recall the two parts of 'mission-with', this would correspond to the first one: 'presence-among'. I now move on to describe a number of projects that I have been involved in as a direct result of living where I have been living. This relates to the second part of 'mission-with', which builds on the first: 'project-praxis', and these projects can be seen as case studies.

None of these activities, for which I am claiming a missional element, could in any sense be regarded as church-led initiatives. Rather, they are community-led – and, importantly, community empowering – with, particularly in the case of Carisma, complete openness for local church support and involvement.

Responding to gang violence:
Carisma and PeaceWeek

Carisma, with its main activity, PeaceWeek, was a long-term community response to a gang violence issue affecting all of inner-south Manchester.[1] It was during a PeaceWeek event in 2005, referred to in the introduction, that I first heard the phrase 'mission-with'. This was to mark the start of a process of reflection on work which, by that time, I had already been doing for nearly three years. So, as a case study of 'project-praxis' it takes in my involvement with Carisma from its beginning in 2002 to its closing in 2015, during which time my thinking on 'mission-with' began and evolved. It is in part a reflection back on those first three years, looking for elements of what would be formulated as a 'mission-with' model, and in part reflection on praxis since, with a more conscious awareness of 'mission-with' as the model was developing.

A snapshot of my evolving thinking can be seen in a paper I gave in late 2007, reflecting on, at that time, five years with Carisma:

> What is different about what I am doing now to other community projects, or indeed Christian outreaches, that I have been involved in? (For a start, no training, prayer meetings, posters, invitation cards to special services.) Isn't mission something

we as Christians do *for* the community? Can this be regarded as mission or is it inferior in some way? Most local churches seem to be uncomfortable with the concept and reluctant to get involved; why? What does it imply for the way the church traditionally sees and does 'mission'?[2]

Gangstop

We had been aware of the gangs and guns problem in the predominantly African-Caribbean Moss Side area for some years. By the late 1990s it had spread into our Chorlton-on-Medlock area with a number of incidents in or near The Groves, which made us concerned local residents and parents. The early-hours arrest of two suspects in our yard, referred to earlier, could be said to be a literal awakening, but there were also other incidents, such as a wounded young man being chased by two others with guns and breaking into and taking refuge in a house just behind ours. One of our daughters was within minutes of a daytime drive-by shooting that left a young man dead.[3]

When we heard about Gangstop, a public march and rally organised on 1st June 2002 by two local young men[4] after a spate of shootings, we went along as a family. It began in Whitworth Park, a central location between Moss Side and Longsight, and significant as a place of meeting, particularly for young people from the two areas who were very nervous about going into the 'other side'. The route took in the areas where most violence had occurred in previous years – Moss Side, Hulme, Rusholme, Longsight, Ardwick – including Chorlton-on-Medlock – and Brunswick, before returning to the park for a rally. I was impressed that a number of members of local churches were involved and that one of the speakers was the pastor of a local Seventh Day Adventist church (though I later discovered he lived in Bolton – about 12 miles away). Another speaker who got my attention was a brave young man who tried to address the crowd on behalf of the gangs, pleading for some understanding of the reasons young men were being drawn into them. One phrase, 'the only time anyone listens to me is when I point a gun at them', was to become foundational for Carisma.[5] Around 400 local people went on the march, together with the Lord Mayor, local MP Tony Lloyd, Bishop of Manchester Christopher Mayfield and local councillors, and it received good media coverage.[6]

The march and rally were planned as a one-off, with no real thought given to any sort of follow-up. However, on the day there was a clear demand for further community action, which was to result in a series of community meetings. Interestingly, those who came to the first meeting wanted a local church leader to give a lead, but no one was willing – or in the room. This indicated to me an openness in the African-Caribbean community for church involvement (the expectation would be to see leaders, that is clergy, pastors, ministers, who were held in respect by all in that community, whether members of their congregations or not). The opportunity that was not taken on this occasion was to prove the first of many. Les Isaac, a church leader from London whose Guns Off Our Street event[7] had helped prompt Gangstop, ended up chairing the process. He describes an exchange at a subsequent meeting:

Towards the end I took a question from the floor: 'Why are you, someone who is based in London, chairing this meeting?' Good question: I explained that many people had asked me to come, and that I had come at my own expense. 'Why had not a local church leader convened this meeting?' the questioner continued. 'You need to go and ask them that,' I replied.[8]

At one point we organised a meeting just for church leaders, which Les drove up from London to lead: the turnout was embarrassingly small.

Out of a series of these community meetings over several months, a new grass-roots community organisation called Carisma emerged, consisting entirely of local people, of which I was one.

Carisma, which stands for Community Alliance for Renewal, Inner-South Manchester Area, was formally launched on 27th November 2002. The remit of the alliance could be summarised in three words:

- **Networking:** mapping and evaluating existing projects and provision and linking them both together and to need.

- **Advocacy:** developing our own voice to engage with media, government, funders and police to counter the 'Gunchester' label and the stigmatising of our young people.

- **Mobilising:** encouraging local people to get involved in positive action. 'All that is necessary for the triumph of evil is that good people do nothing.'[9]

A statement of purpose for Carisma was agreed: 'Life-chances for young people in the community.' This deliberately expressed the underlying positive ethos of the new organisation. To counter what we perceived as the default negative approach of agencies such as the police and the local council – very much governed by the pressure to bring down crime figures, and which saw our young people as needing to be 'diverted' away from something – we deliberately took an alternative, balancing view. This was that there needed to be positive, realistic and compelling alternatives for young people to be diverted *towards*. If they had these 'life-chances',[10] lessening the negative behaviour would, to a large extent, take care of itself. Our default position was to view our young people in a positive way, as individuals with gifts and potential and not collectively as a problem to be solved. As a first step this meant recognising and publicising the simple fact that most of them, most of the time, were not running around with drugs, guns and knives. We were also keen to see that young people were not dealt with in isolation but in their contexts. These were both social: family, school, peer-group, community, employers; and sociological: perception, discrimination, (under) achievement. Or, anything that could help or hinder their access to 'life-chances'.

On getting involved

I went to Gangstop as a local resident concerned to do something. Also, as a Christian, I felt it important that I should be standing with those who had obviously suffered, whether through bereavement, injury, fear for themselves or for a loved one. I was also aware that there were issues of injustice and prejudice mixed in with the gang problem, especially for young black men who, involved or not – and most were not – were being stereotyped and labelled. Beyond attending the march I had no plans to do anything more, but when a follow-up community meeting was announced, as yet with no time or venue, I went straight over to give my details. Initially, beyond seeing this as an opportunity to stand with other concerned local people in some way, I had no thoughts about starting or running anything, just to go along and see if I could join in or offer to help. At the time I had no conscious conception of this being a valid expression of mission, but reflecting back later, what I would now see as hallmarks of a 'mission-with' approach were present.

I got involved as one of a number of fellow residents who shared a concern about a vital issue in our community that was affecting us all. In my case, my motivation was influenced by my Christian faith. While this was also true of some of the others, people of other faiths and none were also involved.

I was not in charge or in control of what was happening, just one voice among many. This could not be described as 'mission' in terms of the Church taking the initiative and doing something 'for' or involving overt taking the gospel 'to' the community. The initiative had come from within, and was owned by, the local community itself, and an opportunity was there to join in as an equal partner and co-worker *with* others.

This indigenous movement was about the common good of the community and taking positive action for the sake of the welfare and well-being of our young people. These are aspects of biblical *shalom*, and marks of the kingdom of God, so therefore for myself as a Christian, this was mission praxis (given a sufficiently wide definition of what is and is not mission), one enacted alongside and with others in equal partnership.

This sharing of power with and working as one of the group, rather than being in charge, could potentially involve risks should the group decide on a course of action that I as a Christian would have problems with following. The safety and control of being the initiator and manager of a project operating from a local church base are lost through working in this way. In writing about 'Mission from the margins' – the place that the Church increasingly occupies in a post-Christendom era – Murray uses the term 'playing away', as we are no longer on safe 'home' ground. He includes engaging with the agenda of others as a strategy and quotes Ann Morisy's model of 'community ministry' as an example of praxis which 'removes power dynamics from the equation, as Christians become fellow strugglers, rather than sources of superior knowledge or virtue'.[11]

Early activities: The Memorial Service and first PeaceWeek

The Carisma Core Group's first meeting on 10th February 2003 had a definite sense of 'OK, what do we do now?' about it. Fortunately, several ideas had already been put forward, including a memorial service for those who had lost loved ones to gang violence. This was envisaged as a one-off and also designed for the community to draw a line under the past and seek to move on. As with Gangstop, it seemed to touch a nerve and grew from a small local affair to a city-wide event in Manchester Cathedral, with more than 500 attending, including civic dignitaries, and attracting much media attention. As the central act, 'pictures of young men murdered in Moss Side, Longsight and surrounding areas were displayed as relatives lit candles, read poems and sang songs'.[12] As names of some 40 of the deceased were read out, a friend or family member laid a single flower at the front. Local school and gospel choirs provided music, the Reverend Joel Edwards, then National Director of the Evangelical Alliance, spoke, and Les Isaac and the recently arrived new Bishop of Manchester, Nigel McCulloch, led prayers. The Bishop wrote later of his impressions:

> One of the first services I attended in Manchester Cathedral was in remembrance of the many young people gunned to death in the city in the previous few years. Etched vividly on my memory are the images of plain-clothes police, discreetly armed, in the aisles; the rival families together in grief and prayer; and pictures of the murdered youngsters placed like icons beside the altar.[13]

Camera crews were asked to remain outside. It was a moving and significant event, and had the unforeseen and unintended consequence of putting Carisma firmly 'on the map' in the eyes of the authorities and media. This began to open doors for the advocacy aspect of our work.

Unfortunately, despite a lot of effort, including individual letters of invitation and my being interviewed on the local BBC radio Sunday programme, only a few local or other church leaders came.

In the early planning for the Memorial Service it had been suggested we should have a Peace Week of activities leading up to it. By January nothing really had been progressed and with not long to go to the service, several of the group, myself included, thought there was not sufficient time to organise this as well. However, I had reckoned without the energy and passion of people with a vision to make things happen, seemingly out of thin air. The first Peace Week, or 'PeaceWeek' as it became known, ran from February 23rd to March 1st and consisted of a few school assemblies and two events called Generating Peace where people of all ages were encouraged to come together to hear and celebrate young people sing, dance, rap and read poems on the theme of peace.

In that first year we also established an office in 'The Saltshaker', formerly the Pepperhill pub and base of one of the gangs. It had been closed by the police and taken over by St Edmund's Church who ran it as a community centre. They let us use it on a generous 'pay-what-you-can' basis.

Growing and developing

By late 2003 we had secured a bit of funding to pay a part-time support worker, whose memorable first day featured a breakdown of the heating system, a jammed burglar alarm and a phone call from the office of Conservative Party leader Michael Howard requesting a meeting.

Having someone in the office to answer calls, organise us and network with different groups and bodies around the area made a big difference to the capacity of the organisation, and we were fortunate in having a worker in Claire who was enthusiastic, committed and a self-starter. She worked with us until 2006, and then stayed on for several more years as a Core Group member and PeaceWeek volunteer. Claire also was able to work on a personal level with quite a few people, using the knowledge that Carisma was building up of the provision available to link people to courses or projects that could help them.

Using the Saltshaker we began what would be a series of community meetings, sometimes with visiting politicians. Over the years these were to include Michael Howard, Tony Blair (while Prime Minister), Alan Johnson (while Home Secretary) and Stephen Timms MP, at the time a Cabinet Minister.

We established relationships with local city councillors and press and media, and also working partnerships with other local activists and organisations. I got to know some remarkable people, not least an amazing Christian called Patsy McKie. Patsy's son Dorrie was shot and killed in 1999, and as a result she felt called by God to set up Mothers Against Violence, a campaigning, caring and mentoring organisation, that we worked alongside on many occasions.

I had kept in touch with Les Isaac and was aware that he wanted to start what he called a 'response from the Church to urban problems'. On a couple of his visits to Manchester he and I had walked the streets of Moss Side late at night talking to people, particularly young people, about what they were concerned about. He was doing similar soundings in London, and in spring 2003 Les invited me to the initial launch meeting of Street Pastors – an initiative to recruit and train volunteers from the churches to patrol the streets at night to 'listen, care and help'.[14] Street Pastors has since expanded to nearly 300 projects in all sorts of contexts, but back then it was a response to the gun and gang problem. Later that year Les contacted me about starting Street Pastors in Moss Side, using Carisma as a facilitating organisation for the initial setting up. The others agreed, and meetings with the police and council and church leaders, who on this occasion were supportive, led to Manchester Street Pastors launching in June 2004, with training and patrols starting soon afterwards.

In the ensuing years, Carisma continued to develop in its role of networking, mobilising and advocacy, working with the media and representing the community on several Independent Advisory Groups and other statutory bodies and platforms and, when appropriate, taking the initiative, either setting up projects or partnering with others where we saw a gap. As well as Street Pastors, examples included working with the Home Office and local police on Stop and Search consultations and role-plays (where young people and police officers swapped places), and Guns to Goods – recycling metal from seized weapons in partnership with the police and Salford University. In 2007 the organisation received the Queen's Award for Voluntary Service, and in 2008 one of our group, local activist Erinma Bell, was awarded an MBE.

As an organisation, Carisma always had a tension between an aspiration to be well organised, strategically thought through and proactive, and the unpredictability and immediacy of the reality of day-to-day life in the inner city of Manchester. This introduced elements of chaos, short-term bodging, unreliability and being reactive and responsive to events, which actually reflects the nature of the context and can sometimes be incredibly powerful, if occasionally frustrating to those like me who tended to hanker after the aforesaid aspirations!

PeaceWeek

The first, hastily arranged, PeaceWeek had worked well and we decided to do it again, now with Claire, our support worker, to help with the organisation. The model began to form of a time and platform for anyone – individuals, groups, faith groups, voluntary and statutory organisations, schools, businesses – to join in by participating in the centrally organised events and activities, or creating their own. It was about 'generating good news in an area known for bad', a phrase I came up with to use in our publicity. The use of the term 'good news' is an intentional allusion to building *shalom*, and to the gospel. Through education, celebration, advocacy, and creative and positive messages and activities the aim was to increase well-being and confidence in individuals and, through that, community cohesion (to pick up some of the council's terminology). Over the next nine years, PeaceWeek, as it became known, grew to become a fixture every spring, encompassing a range of activities and events. These included:

- A Family March for Peace which took place at dusk lit by lanterns made by local children in schools or workshops. There were starting points in Longsight and Moss Side, finishing with a rally in a central place such as a park, the two 'sides' meeting up, so challenging the territorial rivalry that was a feature of the gang violence.

- 'The Launch Event'. The first night of PeaceWeek was given over to local young people to sing, dance, rap and act as a showcase to the world that there was as much talent here as anywhere else. This grew out of our rather amateur Generating Peace events and is a case of how much better something can be when people who know what they are doing get involved as partners – a good example of how the PeaceWeek dynamic worked.

- Long before the more recent wider acknowledgement, local community members recognised that risk of gang involvement began at a young age for a number of young people, particularly boys. So each PeaceWeek included a programme of assemblies, classes and workshops in local primary schools, sometimes with a creative project such as peace mosaics for a local park, a book of poems and artwork, or recording a CD of peace-themed songs and occasionally a Showcase event if resources permitted. To cover as many schools as possible we worked with other groups such as Mothers Against Violence and pulled together a team of people for which, thanks to my previous work in schools with YFC, I was able to provide some basic dos and don'ts training.

Walsh wrote about our schools work:

> Their hardest task will be rooting out the gang culture now it has become ingrained. Members of the anti-gang community group CARISMA have begun to take their message to primary schools because they found that by the time the children reach secondary school, it is too late. One member gave a presentation to students aged thirteen and fourteen. 'I asked them to come up with reasons for joining a gang, and they had no trouble filling the flip chart,' she said. 'Then I asked how they would get the money to buy an expensive piece of jewellery if they did not turn to crime, and they struggled. That is scary. And those weren't bad kids – they were just average.' That is how deeply the gang lifestyle is ingrained.[15]

- In 2008 we introduced a peace awards dinner in a city centre hotel and with a celebrity guest. Called the OSBAs (Outstanding Social Behaviour Awards – a deliberate play on ASBO) these were designed to recognise positive contributions to the community, as opposed to negative ones, with each award sponsored by a business or charity. The awards were well reported each year in the local *Manchester Evening News*, and sometimes got a bit of national coverage.

- For three years we ran a community radio station, PeaceFM, as a four-week RSL (Restricted Service Licence). This proved so successful that an application to OFCOM in 2009 for a five-year licence was successful. Music, radio and DJ-ing are very popular parts of the local African-Caribbean culture (seen in the long and normally benignly tolerated tradition of pirate radio in Moss Side), and this station also fulfilled another part of our advocacy remit in that it, quite literally, gave a voice to local people.

- The PeaceWeek Shield was an annual sports tournament, usually five-a-side football, bringing together primarily young people from different areas, and often featuring an exhibition match with teams from the police or PeaceFM DJs.

- In 2006, in partnership with the police, we implemented a request from the community for a weapons amnesty, calling it 'Good Riddance'. Making this work actually involved a lot of effort behind the scenes by local police officers as it turned out that technically what we were proposing was outside of the then current legislation. The fix was to call it a 'hand-in' instead and get a special dispensation from the Home Office. This has since been used as a template for similar schemes in other parts of the country.

- Other initiatives included a PeaceWeek newspaper, produced in partnership with local charity Healthy Ardwick (15,000 copies were distributed around the area),[16] and producing crime-scene incident tape with the message 'Work, hope, pray, long for Peace'.

- On a few occasions displays of photographs or art with a bearing on peace and images of the community have been shown in local supermarkets, churches and libraries.

Partnership was important, and events and activities arranged for PeaceWeek by or in partnership with other groups and organisations included: music and poetry evenings, Family Comedy Night, the Peace Lecture, a community clean-up, Community Fun Days, Student Action day, community meetings, breakfasts, debates and *Question Time*-style panels with local police, councillors and MPs.

We also made links with similar initiatives in other cities, including London Week of Peace[17] and 'Together for Peace'[18] in Leeds. The London week takes place in September so we were able to visit to observe and exchange ideas and resources and also have its director Rev Nims Obunge as a guest at our Peace Week on several occasions.

Every year local churches and faith groups were encouraged, along with every other grouping and organisation, to get involved by supporting the core events, but also by creating their own events and activities, or simply by having a peace-related theme for already existing ones. Events that resulted included peace-themed Sunday services, a Leaders' Lunch, a breakfast for church leaders and local MPs, a 24-hours of prayer for peace, a peace vigil, buildings opened for reflection and prayer, an ecumenical peace service, a Buddhist musical evening and a Baha'i event involving meditations and music. There will probably have been others that we were not aware of, but over the ten years of PeaceWeek the level of involvement observed from the faith sector was minimal, with several of the main churches of the area not participating at all.

Our local MP Tony Lloyd (and to a lesser extent Gerald Kaufman from the next constituency when we had events there), along with most local ward councillors and several senior council staff, were fully supportive of PeaceWeek, and of Carisma as an organisation. Recognising and encouraging local initiative, they would often attend and take part in events, sometimes at short notice, and would advocate for us in the background. I've been able to carry over some of the relationships into other projects.

Positive relationships with the media grew, and local newspapers, radio and television became much more receptive to reporting good news stories we brought to them. From PeaceWeek these included our OSBA Awards Dinner, PeaceFM, the Lantern Parade and stunts such as wrapping churches, schools and other buildings across the city in rolls of our peace-themed incident-tape![19]

Relating to the police

One of the early issues to be reckoned with in Carisma was the community's suspicion of the police, which was reflected within the Core Group. There was some resistance to my acceptance of an invitation to be a founder member of an Independent Advisory Group (IAG) for Manchester Multi-Agency Gang Strategy (MMAGS). This had been set up in 2001 as an imaginative project, unique in the United Kingdom, based on Operation Ceasefire, a much-praised scheme started in 1996 in Boston in the United States.[20] It was based upon the different agencies dealing with young people – in, or at risk of joining, gangs – working closely together in a 'joined-up' strategy. Interestingly, one significant partner-group of Operation Ceasefire not included in MMAGS was the churches. This could have been because there is no equivalent network in Manchester to Boston's Ten Point Coalition of 43 black-led churches.[21] Though the police were only one of the partner agencies, MMAGS was initially perceived in the community as being no more than a police-led front for intelligence-gathering. I resolved the issue by joining as an individual resident, but as time went on members of the Core Group began to meet and get to know a number of senior police officers who, it was clear, were also deeply committed to solving this problem.

We grew to realise that not all police were the same and that the community's default position of suspicion, though understandable, given many past examples of injustice, had to be challenged.[22] Also, like it or not, the police, the council and other statutory organisations were part of the equation and had to be related to and worked with, though not uncritically (one of our members once refused to let a senior police officer start a meeting until he had promised to look into the wrongful arrest of a young black man the night before).

Reflecting back now it is clear that this involvement was a factor in breaking down an antipathy towards the police. In the ensuing years others from Carisma joined other IAGs and we undertook joint projects with the police, came to appreciate the commitment and hard work of many officers and built up close relationships with some senior officers.

Peacemaking

Not everything about Carisma was positive and successful. As I got to know the community in Moss Side and developed relationships and friendships with a number of people who were part of the various activities and organisations, I became aware of some of the undercurrents and fault lines that run through any group of people. One or more of these contributed to a power struggle for PeaceFM, triggered by a physical confrontation at the station when an argument about how it was being run boiled over.

Though I helped set up PeaceFM when it got its five-year licence, I was not involved in the running of the station, but knew many of the people who were. As word of the incident spread, together with two very different versions of what had happened with accusations and counter-accusations flying, two groups quickly formed, each seeking to establish their version as the truth.

I began to be contacted by people from both groups asking for meetings. This was at least partly to recruit me to their 'side', but I always agreed to meet and listen. My intention was not to be drawn into taking sides but to try to stay in positive relationship with each individual and, when possible, to reflect back opposing views and push for reconciliation. There was a definite issue with the governance of the station, but also a battle to take control of what was seen as a lucrative and attractive community asset. My concern was more to do with the broken relationships, to say nothing of the harm such a dispute could do at a community radio station with 'peace' in its name and supposed to be promoting harmony!

After a long process, the governance issue was sorted out, which involved the replacement of the old directors, something I think had more to do with the power struggle and relationship breakdown. Meanwhile I had persuaded the Carisma trustees to put up the first £1,000 of fees for a Third Sector Professional Mediation agency run by a Christian I knew who would offer to meet with individuals from either group and seek to bring about reconciliation. Unfortunately no one took up the offer, and we were left with a situation where a number of valuable and talented individuals were lost to PeaceFM and also to Carisma and PeaceWeek.

Reflecting on my role in this, it is interesting that as a white Christian I was trusted with a peacemaking and brokering role in this affair, and it says something about the credibility I had managed to build up through my years of involvement, based on more years of living locally. However, it is a shame that, while PeaceFM survived the crisis,[23] my efforts at encouraging personal reconciliation were ultimately unsuccessful. During this time I had to confront and disagree with some people that I had worked with for a long time and would count as friends. It is possible that a situation could have arisen where I was misunderstood or perceived to be siding with one or other parties in the conflict, which could have damaged my relationships with others. Working with others always carries the risk of having to withdraw for reasons of principle or rejection. Thankfully, that did not happen, unsatisfactory as the outcome of this situation was in other ways.

Mission accomplished?

From 2008 there was a marked decrease in gun crime, which so far has been sustained. The police and media credited community action (not just by Carisma) as playing an important part.[24] This meant that we stopped PeaceWeek in 2012 and then closed Carisma in 2015, the trustees having decided, probably rightly, 'mission accomplished'. It was true that the problem of gang-based violence to which we had set up in response was much improved, and the context had changed, good news indeed. But several of us felt – and still feel – that more work on the causes behind those symptoms remains to be done,[25] maybe through a new 'son of Carisma' organisation: also grass roots.[26] Unfortunately, funding seems to go with headlines, and that, together with several other factors, including fatigue, and a feeling among local people of 'problem solved', closed that door. Such is 'mission-with' 'project-praxis': you're not in charge and you go with the majority.

---

[1] For a longer, more detailed account of the forming and activities of Carisma, see my 'Carisma: The First Ten Years' which can be downloaded from http://www.urbanpresence.org.uk/Carisma10.pdf (accessed 5th October 2016). Appendices 2 and 3 describe the rise of the gang issue, its context and background and responses to it.

[2] Paul Keeble, 'Mission With'. Paper presented at the Urban Theology Collective, Hawarden, North Wales, December 2007.

[3] I have written about this at greater length. Paul Keeble, 'Gang Violence', in Eastman and Latham, eds., *Urban Church*.

[4] Michael McFarquhar and Gary Gordon. 'At the last funeral we looked around. There were hundreds of people there, and we thought "Why do you only get this level of community spirit at funerals? It's time to do something about it".' *The Guardian*, 22nd April 2002.

[5] Also referred to by Peter Walsh in *Gang War: The Inside Story of the Manchester Gangs* (Reading: Milo, 2003) p.319.

[6] 'No-one here is kidding themselves that this march will put an instant stop to the gun culture here in Moss Side and Longsight, but the organisers say it is an important first step in bringing the communities together in showing their opposition to the violence.' BBC TV report. One of the BBC interviewees was our then 13-year-old daughter Alannah.

[7] 'Two black church leaders in Britain, Les Isaac and David Shoshanya, have been instrumental in trying to bring gun violence onto the church agenda. Together with a policeman, Ian Crichlow, they launched the "Guns Off Our Streets" campaign in May last year. They visited churches in London, Birmingham and Manchester to raise the awareness of congregations about the issue as well as to give them strategies to deal with it.' Marcia Dixon, 'Guns and the Cross', *The Tablet*, 11th January 2003. I had actually met and worked with Les a few times in the 1980s and it was good to renew our friendship.

[8] Les Isaac with Rosalind Davies, *Street Pastors* (Eastbourne: David C. Cook, 2009) p.178.

[9] Attributed to Edmund Burke (1729–97) with his original 'men' altered to 'people'. This phrase was used on all of Carisma's publicity.

[10] 'A Weberian term that designates a person's chances of acquiring economic, cultural, and social goods.' C. Calhoun, ed, *Dictionary of the Social Sciences* (Oxford: University Press, 2002) p.274. Denial of access to life-chances is seen as a result of passive social exclusion.

[11] Stuart Murray, *Church After Christendom* (Milton Keynes: Paternoster, 2004) p.159.

[12] Walsh, *Gang War*, p.306. Also referred to in Les Isaac with Rosalind Davies, *Street Pastors*, pp.180–181.

[13] Nigel McCulloch, 'The Quiet Ministry of Support Carries On', *The Church Times*, 20th June 2008, http://www.churchtimes.co.uk/articles/2008/20-june/comment/the-quiet-ministry-of-support-carries-on (accessed 6th October 2016).

[14] www.streetpastors.org.uk (accessed 20th January 2017).

[15] Walsh, *Gang War*, p.322. Despite correctly noting we worked in primary schools, Walsh actually gets the age of the children wrong – they would have been Year 6, ie ten or eleven years old.

[16] There is a pdf download of this at: http://www.urbanpresence.org.uk/carisma/images/pw2012/pw12_web.pdf (accessed 24th January 2017).

[17] Now JCI London Peace Week. http://www.londonpeaceweek.org (accessed 31st October 2016).

[18] http://www.t4p.org.uk (accessed 31st October 2016).

[19] *Manchester Evening News*, 18th February 2012, http://menmedia.co.uk/manchestereveningnews/news/s/1485847_police-tape-to-be-swapped-for-peace-tape-when-festival-gets-underway (accessed 5th October 2016).

[20] https://www.hks.harvard.edu/programs/criminaljustice/research-publications/gangs-guns-urban-violence/operation-ceasefire-boston-gun-project (accessed 5th October 2016).

[21] 'The streets are much safer. The collaboration between the black churches and the police has produced results unseen in any other city.' The Reverend Eugene Rivers, co-founder of the Ten Point Coalition, a network of 43 black churches in Boston. Quoted in Sam Allis, 'How to Start a Ceasefire: Learning from Boston', *Time Magazine*, 21st July 1997,

http://www.time.com/time/magazine/article/0,9171,986710-1,00.html (accessed 5th October 2016).

[22] For British-born black and Asian young people through the 1970s, Fryer records persistent racist attitudes in education, housing, employment and the police, and catalogues a number of significant incidents of racially motivated attacks and injustice in their handling by the police and courts. P. Fryer, *Staying Power: The History of Black People in Britain* (London: Pluto Press, 1984).

[23] History is written by the winners. While the station is still going strong, the name has since been changed and its birth out of PeaceWeek has been all but forgotten.

[24] 'Chief Constable Peter Fahy said Manchester has shed its "Gunchester" image thanks to the police and community efforts to tackle gangs.' *Manchester Evening News*, 7th July 2011. This article gives an overview of Moss Side 30 years on from the 1981 riots.

'Ten percent of our success is due to police work – the other ninety percent is due to a well functioning teamwork with local politicians, social authorities and local street organisations.' Det. Chief Supt. Dave Keller, interviewed in *Politiken.dk*, 8th May 2009.

'The sudden drop in gun crime in Manchester is down to more than just good policing. Communities deserve praise too. … Above all, we should not underestimate the efforts of communities themselves to address these problems … In the most crime-ravaged areas of the city, groups like Mothers Against Violence and Carisma, under the inspirational guidance of Erinma Bell, have made monumental efforts to empower communities to stand up to the gangs.' Ally Fogg, 'Gunchester no more?', *The Guardian*, 3rd February 2009, http://www.guardian.co.uk/commentisfree/2009/feb/03/gun-crime-manchester-communities-police (accessed 5th October 2016).

[25] 'The solutions to gun and gang crime are not as simple as just catching the bad guys, even though that is an essential component. If the streets on which they grow continue to fertilise criminality and violence, then we are merely cutting off the nettles, not pulling up the roots.' Ally Fogg, *The Guardian*, 3rd February 2009.

[26] Erinma Bell continues to work with the community in Moss Side through local charity Chrysalis, and some projects such as community radio station PeaceFM (now known as Legacy FM) and Guns to Goods are still going. As a nice postscript to my work with Carisma, I recently attended the unveiling of a bust of Erinma made from recycled gun metal. This took place at Manchester Cathedral, the venue for our Memorial Service in 2003.

Local Community Organising

The other three projects I want to describe are more local to Chorlton-on-Medlock, and can be seen as expressions of Local Community Organising. Each was an issue we were affected by personally, along with other local residents. These are on a much smaller scale than Carisma or PeaceWeek (which share some features of Community Organising) but nevertheless also illustrate characteristics of 'mission-with' 'project-praxis'.

I wrote earlier about Judith and I organising the residents of our block of flats to get a broken lift fixed, only to discover much later I had been using some methods of Community Organising. Back then, in 1982, though seeking to live as what I would come to call a 'presence-among' in the community, I had no real conception of 'mission-with' as 'project-praxis' and was operating in a 'mission-to' and 'mission-for' mode. The difference with the projects below is that they came much later and my thinking had moved on.

The first project, working with others to improve our local park, began at around the same time as Carisma, and, as that developed, the notion of *shalom*-building 'project-praxis' that grew out of it can also be reflected in how I saw this involvement. The other two – Residents' Car Parking and the Community Garden – began after I had learned more about Community Organising, already had several years' experience working with Carisma and PeaceWeek and had started to formulate my thinking on this second stage of 'mission-with'. So the praxis and reflection on it are with an awareness of what was evolving as the 'project-praxis' stage of the 'mission-with' model.

Community Organising in various forms can be traced back to the nineteenth century, but the modern form, with a political and campaigning edge, was largely developed from the late 1930s by Saul Alinsky. He saw it as a way of addressing social problems by getting individuals affected by them motivated to take action. By pooling their resources and power to make a whole greater than the sum of its parts, they could challenge dominant and oppressive political powers. It has been defined as:

> a democratically-governed, values-driven process that catalyzes the power of individuals to work collectively to make the changes they want to see in their communities. Community organizers honor and develop the leadership potential in everyday people by helping them identify problems and solutions, and then by supporting them as they take action to make those solutions a reality.[1]

As such, Community Organising and 'mission-with' share values such as working with, empowering and partnership.

Friends of Swinton Grove Park

In 2002 a council strategy to encourage local people to take an interest in the upkeep of Manchester's parks resulted in a meeting about setting up a Friends group for the small park near us off Swinton Grove. Judith and I had taken our children there many times but the state of it left a lot to be desired – broken or vandalised equipment, litter and dog mess, sometimes used needles and condoms. At some point, as a result of a European Safety Directive, the swings and other equipment had been deemed 'unsafe' and instead of being replaced had simply been removed, further reducing use of the park. Only a few of us attended the meeting, but it was enough for council officials to fudge through the forming of a Friends of Swinton Grove Park group,[2] and with it the ticking of another outputs box. Despite this inauspicious beginning, the group began to gel together well with each other and with Kirsty, our initial link person from Manchester Leisure.

Over the years since, funding has been found for substantial improvements such as new play and all-weather sports areas, bins, benches, plants, railings, and signs. An annual Fun Day attracts several hundred people, and unusually for Manchester has never been rained off! Our church has given substantial assistance to this day in recent years – loan of tables, chairs, minibus and the vicar as DJ and bingo caller. The park is now heavily used by local people and has been awarded a 'Green Flag'.

When this project began, I probably saw it as what I would now describe as a piece of 'mission-for' coming out of our 'presence-among'. We were joining with other local residents to improve our park. As my contemporaneous work with PeaceWeek led to a rethinking of my conception of mission to include *shalom*-building – and that by whoever was doing it, whether they saw it that way or not

– so too my perception of this project shifted. Improving the park has been another bit of *shalom*, a positive end in itself, and another way of getting to know people and work alongside them. As with Carisma, it is a situation where we are not in charge but are members of a group working together on a specific project. This is partnership and a sharing of power, and as such involves some risk.

> The most profoundly incarnational acts are those where we, as individuals or churches, not only serve our communities, but do so in projects we don't own and don't control – for, in the end, incarnation is fundamentally about giving up control.[3]

There was once a situation where, after agreeing to hire a firm to provide the food for the Fun Day, another offering a better price was found. Some members of the group were all for telling the first company that the event had been cancelled or our funding cut, so we could hire the second. Judith and I objected to this on the grounds that it was deceitful and could cause the group problems if the lie was discovered. The group agreed and the arrangement remained as it was. What if the other view had prevailed? That may have been an occasion to exercise the power we had to withdraw from the group. However, I think people, with encouragement, are more than willing to do the right thing, especially if someone is willing to break ranks and voice their objection to a dubious proposal that needs group solidarity to prop up its shaky justification.

One writer refers, perhaps slightly dramatically, to a 'no-man's land that exists between church and community', but draws out an advantage of good relationships in such situations:

> When good groups and personal relationships have been established, the moments of crisis of conscience are moments of enormous educational value. People who do not share a Christian's view feel great responsibility towards a proven friend who is being driven into a conscience corner and will generally seek, and often find, a way out for him.[4]

Residents' car parking

In this campaign there was an additional element in that we were trying to get the council to do something. This puts it more in common with full-blown 'Community Organising' initiatives which concentrate more on a political agenda seeking to change policies that adversely affect people.[5]

Two factors had caused a large increase in the numbers of non-residents parking on The Groves in 2007. The first was the introduction of a residents' parking scheme on the road at the bottom of The Groves, between us and Manchester's biggest hospital, which meant that our streets now provided the nearest free parking for visitors and staff. The second was a major redevelopment of the hospital which reduced existing parking space there, and led to a large number of contractors' vehicles arriving every day. The hospital initially had a map on its website showing contractors local places to park – including The Groves. This was quickly removed when our campaign started.

Within weeks of the start of the adjacent restricted parking, The Groves were crammed full of cars, vans and minibuses. Stories began to circulate. Apart from grumblings about not being able to park outside one's own house, there were more problematical issues and car and non-car owners were both being affected. A disabled person on East Grove had to walk 50 yards to his car; the minibus that collected and returned a child with special needs every day was unable to get close; bins were not emptied as the lorry could not get access; deliveries were not made; families visiting parents and grandparents struggled to park. For us, apart from delivery and collection issues, it was often having to park several streets away – particularly in the rain – or blocking the road while we took the shopping in. The fire brigade attended an incident one Saturday and said if it had been a weekday they would have had problems getting access for the engine.

Some individuals began to make complaints, but got no response. Others 'acquired' traffic cones, or used bins and other objects to protect 'their' space – illegally. Frustration was increasing, and one or two confrontations had taken place. After a number of conversations with disgruntled neighbours I saw an opportunity to apply some of what I had been learning recently about Community Organising.[6]

One of the ideals behind Community Organising is to combine the little bit of power we each have to make a bigger impact together. Several of us took a survey door-to-door to record people's feelings and their stories, and to get their thoughts on further action we could take. A public meeting with the local councillors, the healthcare trust and contractors was felt to be a good next step. Suggestions of barricading The Groves with our wheelie bins and letting down tyres were duly noted under 'possible options if the meeting doesn't work'. The survey results and copies of the originals (not the originals because things get lost) were sent to the councillors and the local Ward Coordinator and a venue booked and date set for the meeting. I started a website to track the progress of the issue (I suspect this was visited more by the council and some transport activists than residents, but that was useful in itself). We also produced a printed sheet reminding everyone about the meeting and that, to borrow a saying that had become popular at Carisma meetings, 'Decisions are made by those who turn up.' Even with that advice I had a couple of conversations along the lines of, 'You can go on my behalf. I don't know what to say at meetings,' showing the lack of confidence that holds many people back around here. I assured them they would not have to say anything if they did not want to, and that this was an occasion where numbers in the room was important.

Every opportunity was taken to encourage people to turn up, to be respectful and, when the time came, to share the most powerful thing they had – their stories. For the more reticent we had a sheaf of stories from the surveys that could be read out.

I was actually less concerned about the shy as with some of our more vocal residents who could easily turn this into a 'shout at the suits' session. From a previous experience, when a local school was controversially closed down, I had observed that this tactic was counterproductive. However, it is the only one left for some with little confidence or ability to articulate building frustration felt at how 'they' always seem to put 'us' down.

On the day, we watched a group of visibly nervous councillors and council officials looking on as around 60 residents from The Groves arrived. The healthcare trust and contractors declined the invitation, but that apart the meeting was a complete success. The problem was outlined, some told their stories first-hand, and before half an hour had passed we had been promised a residents' parking scheme in principle. Most of the rest of the meeting was taken up with a discussion about permits for visitors, such as the families of some of our older residents. No one shouted. I was able to stay at the back and let people speak for themselves, telling their stories, and then, as confidence grew, make suggestions and comments to the council officers.

Council wheels move slowly and it took nearly two years for the scheme to actually be implemented. It is working well. We had to bite our tongues when the local councillors gave themselves the credit for it.

Working together on the shared issue of parking has had a good effect on The Groves. Many people have got to know others better. People love to tell the story of how we got the council to change its mind, and an important principle has been established: it is possible to make positive change by working together.

There have also been side benefits. Judith and I have a higher profile, though we need to be careful that we do not become the default people for 'getting things done', keeping in mind the Iron Rule of Community Organising: 'Never do for others what they can do for themselves.'[7] We feel very much that the parking campaign was a working *with* rather than *for*, done as far as possible by consensus, which is an important dynamic. It helped that I also knew all of the local councillors and was able to act as a sort of go-between, but the crucial factor was focusing the frustration of a number of people and using that combined energy to positive effect. This was a small piece of empowerment, and therefore a small step closer to God's purpose for His created people of individual and corporate *shalom*. It led directly to another small step through the creation of the Community Garden.

The Community Garden

It was a neighbour who had the idea to do something to improve the communal area, known as The Croft, which four rows of houses, one of which includes ours, back on to. At some point this had been landscaped and planted as a garden area, but by the time we arrived it was rundown and overgrown, used only for dumping, litter, dog mess, drug-taking and drinking.

This was in part a 'What can we do next?' after the parking campaign, and came out of a couple of clean-up days, initiated by a very good environmental officer at the council who had noticed The Croft was in quite a bad way. Houses were leafleted with the dates, and a group of student volunteers and a skip and some tools duly arrived. Judith and I were two of only four residents who joined in, but one who watched for a while from her back gate as the skip filled with litter, debris and weeds saw the potential for the area and began to talk about what could be done next.

The upshot, with some support behind the scenes by Judith and myself, was a Neighbours' Day barbecue in The Croft in June 2010, funded by a £200 council grant. Around 100 adults, children and young people came during the course of a sunny afternoon, between two rainy days, and it was good to see people enjoying themselves and engaging with each other. (The difference in turnout between the council-organised clean-up and locally organised events since can be attributed to local ownership versus wariness of the council, better publicity and, of course, free food!) A short survey form gathered opinions and ideas for how to improve The Croft, and yielded commitments to give some time helping to maintain it. Since then many hours have been put in clearing, planting and weeding, and bids for funding for gates, plants and tools have been successful. We have had more community events, planting and 'Big Dig' sessions, a Jubilee event in the summer of 2012 and more recently several Bring and Share meals.[8] However, the initial enthusiasm for the work of gardening has tailed off to a committed few and could do with a boost.

Our neighbour who had the initial idea has discovered the benefits of taking action yourself rather than expecting 'them' to do something, and has since helped with the Friends of Swinton Grove Park, along with other voluntary work. She is more confident and claims a noticeable improvement in her depression and in a tendency to drink heavily. Her house is a lot tidier and she has redecorated several rooms and made other improvements. She has returned to education through a series of short-term courses and recently she succeeded (where we failed some years ago) in setting up a Neighbourhood Watch scheme with the help of a local community police officer. We have discovered that she used to bring her now grown-up children to the toddler group and youth work at Brunswick Church. As a nice piece of recognition from the council, she (and Judith) were invited to the Queen's Diamond Jubilee Garden Party in Manchester in March 2012.

In this example of 'mission-with' 'project-praxis', we were able to take a lower-profile role, supporting someone else, in our working with others. Again, use was made of some elements of Community Organising, such as leafleting and requests for ideas, but this time at the suggestion of our neighbour. The creation of the garden has had the effect not only of improving our environment, but also of building self-esteem and bringing increased wholeness to a self-confessed one-time 'neighbour from hell'. Another bit of *shalom*, and evidence of God at work in someone's life, which we are hoping she will come to acknowledge at some point.

---

[1] Catherine Crystal Foster and Justin Louie, *Grassroots Action and Learning for Social Change: Evaluating Community Organising* (Washington: Centre for Evaluation Innovation, March 2010), p.2.

[2] http://www.fosgp.org.uk (accessed 20th January 2017).

[3] Steve Chalke, *Intelligent Church: A Journey Towards Christ-centred Community* (Grand Rapids, MI: Zondervan, 2006) p.113.

[4] George Lovell, *The Church and Community Development: An Introduction* (London: Avec Publications, 1972) p.59.

[5] Also the case with a more recent and smaller campaign with the local councillors to get The Groves 'Red-Lined' to limit the number of houses of multiple occupancy and hence the destabilising effect on the community of short-term residents.

[6] I had been doing some research after a Carisma training day had thrown up that what we had been doing partially fitted the Community Organising model.

[7] Linthicum, *Building a People of Power*, p.170.

[8] http://grovesgarden.org.uk (accessed 20th January 2017).

Working with the neighbours: reflections on 'project-praxis'

The examples of 'project-praxis' recounted show clearly the 'mission-with' characteristics of equal partnership and shared *shalom*-building. This is the dynamic Steve Chalke is talking about when he says, 'True incarnation is when I go out and get involved in a local project where I don't run the show and I don't pull all the strings.'[1] It breaks down the us/them, provider/dependent, superior/inferior barriers (whether based on substance or perception or stereotyping) that often come between the community and the Church. It also requires humility and makes the statement that Christians do not have a monopoly on goodness and caring.

To what extent, if any, could I have been involved in the various responses and projects described above had I not been a resident of the local area or member of the communities affected by the issues? A prerequisite for the 'project-praxis' stage of 'mission-with' is 'presence-among'. It cannot be done as effectively – if at all – from a distance. If the issue I am working on with others is not affecting me at least in some ways similar to how it is affecting them, can I really empathise and be motivated in the same way?

It could be speculated how much, if any, of the above would feature in a traditional missionary or evangelist's newsletter. This is praxis on the edges of what could be seen as 'missional', but can be foundational for other, more overtly missional activity based on relationship. However, each project, as a piece of *shalom*-building, is firstly an end in itself.

Carisma and PeaceWeek

My getting involved with a community-led response to the gang violence issue came out of the concern, shared by other parents, about the safety of my family living in this area. However, I did not have the additional issues involved in being black, so the common ground was geographic, if not cultural, closeness.[2] If I were black and living in another place could I be involved as 'mission-with' praxis on a basis of that common ground? Or is there something particular or special about geographic location – being physically present in a particular place at a particular time? As I was to observe on a number of occasions, being there counts far more with local people than promising to pray from a distance.

I believe the importance of location and incarnational identification for Christians cannot be overemphasised, and will return to this in the light of the example of Jesus later. For Gutiérrez, incarnational embodiment of the gospel was crucial, with the Church being a material sign of the presence of Christ with people, particularly the poor, and faith being evidenced by concrete action (orthopraxis), more than verbal assent (orthodoxy). 'Practice is the locus of verification of our faith in God.'[3]

A black person living in a different area could share the concern as they might identify with some of the underlying issues of racism and poverty. A white person living in Didsbury (Manchester's archetypal leafy suburb) could share the concern through having had a son or daughter injured by gang violence, or, as was the position of one of Carisma's trustees, from being the head of a successful school in the Hulme/Moss Side area for many years, now retired. But what would Carisma have looked like – would it have got anywhere – if it had been run by a group of people none of whom lived in the affected area?

Apart from occasional overspills, the gang issue was localised to a specific geographical area with an ethnically mixed population, so concern from white and black African-Caribbean – and Asian – residents is valid as their children walk streets where there is a risk of violence. African-Caribbean residents have an extra ground for concern as many of the gang members are drawn from their young people. There is scope for some involvement from 'outside', but it must serve, not dictate (for example, professional skills maybe not available in the local context, but required for running a charity, such as accounting for the role of treasurer). Being able to identify – knowing *what it is like* to live in an affected area, or to be a part of a stereotyped and disadvantaged ethnic group – is an important basis for praxis. This is an aspect of incarnational ministry: 'For we do not have a high priest who is unable to feel sympathy with our weaknesses'.[4]

Drawing in others with different skills and abilities to enrich the activity and increase ownership and confidence is an example of the partnering characteristic of 'project-praxis' spoken of above. While in doing this it is assumed the concern and vision to take action is shared; this delegation and sharing of power necessarily involves some risk as motives can be mixed and competency may not always be what I, or others, would hope for.

An occasional tension in organising PeaceWeek was between the local culture's way of doing things at the last minute, with lots of energy and passion, and with it, arguably, more integrity to the context, and my middle-class desire to plan in advance. A blend of both works best (but is tricky to achieve), so that if we want to invite the Lord Mayor to an event we do not leave contacting his office until the week before!

There can also be disagreements and power struggles, especially when an initiative is perceived as successful (this became an issue with PeaceFM). But intervention (and reverting to 'for' rather than 'with') – if it is considered at all, or even possible if partnership is truly equal – should be a last resort. Maybe for some local churches the possible risks involved in joining with the local community rather than running an event for them helps explain their reluctance to respond to our invitations.

MMAGS IAG Membership as an expression of 'mission-with'

As mentioned above, as part of my involvement with Carisma I joined the Independent Advisory Group for MMAGS, the Manchester Multi-Agency Gang Strategy.

From a 'mission-with' perspective, what is the difference between myself as a Christian being on this IAG and a non-Christian or a Muslim? In one sense none, as the hope would be that each would strive to fulfil the role well. As a Christian I would ask, where is the mission or gospel or Christian distinctive or 'saltiness' (changing the flavour, to use the image of Matthew 5:13)? By that I do not mean trying to engineer a conversation about the Bible at a coffee break, but in doing the job itself. This is easier to define if it is a church-based or church-run activity such as a job club, or a toddler group, which could be seen as 'mission-for' the community, and easier still if it is a church-based activity with an overt 'spiritual' agenda such as a Children's Holiday Club or a Guest Service – 'mission-to' the community. 'Mission-with' is out in the community, alongside fellow members of that community and with no more power or ownership than anyone else – 'playing away', as Murray puts it.

Being 'missional' at the IAG meeting is a more subtle and nuanced thing. My relating to the group can be seen as personal mission praxis within a 'project-praxis' context. To give some practical examples from my experience: where possible I tried to speak positively about young people and, while not absolving them of responsibility, to remind the group of the wider context of discrimination, disadvantage, stereotyping, lack of role models and a materialistic society that their criminal activity needed to be set in;[5] I encouraged partnership activities with churches and other faith groups, and publicised initiatives churches were involved in; I even commented on how the outdoor events of PeaceWeek invariably seemed to be rain-free (remarkable in Manchester in February/March). This led to several opportunities to engage directly with other members of the group or officers and officials about my faith, often initiated by them, but that was not the end for which taking part in the group was the means. My involvement was also to play a part in initiating positive relationships with the police in a community which initially was very suspicious – not without reason. That is another peacemaking or *shalom*-building outcome, which I would regard in a missional sense, given that we are to 'live in peace with everyone'.[6]

Lovell recognises that in community development, where 'people with different skills and from different disciplines work together', Christians have a unique contribution to make:

> The Christian brings his own skills, his own resources, his own understanding of man's nature and, with these, the resources that are in Christ and the Church. These are resources to be offered at any appropriate point and examined in the same way as any other resources that a community development worker might offer to an autonomous group.[7]

These resources 'in Christ and the Church' will be primarily located around the Christian understanding of the spiritual dimension to human problems and issues and their treatment and solution.

Local Community Organising

All of the local 'mission-with' examples recounted above are specific projects in our immediate neighbourhood where we have taken a lead alongside others or supported someone else. As such they have raised our profile and given us the opportunity both to get to know more people and to deepen existing relationships. But they are all to be set against a background of being local residents and doing the things that local residents do, week in, week out. This is the important ongoing 'mission-with' praxis background foundational to any specific response or project that may come along from time to time.

With the car-parking issue, it is unlikely that I would have heard of this or been motivated to get involved if it was not happening literally on my doorstep. It was causing *us* problems and I was aware that this was the case for others, including more vulnerable neighbours, and that some were taking perhaps unwise remedial action. Because we were in good relationships with our neighbours, as well as also being affected personally by the issue, I was able to discourage these methods and encourage our working together.

Equally for working on the local park and The Croft, we were among those who wanted to improve the local environment and get better places and facilities for our children to play in. This creates individual and shared motivation, ground on which to build relationships, and a common feel-good factor when something is achieved. Both of these projects have involved cooperation with a number of council staff, but helpful as they have been, there is not the same level of joint feeling, as in the final analysis they are doing a job and come in from outside. And their high level of turnover (much worse since 'The Cuts') also leaves little time to build relationships.

In terms of well-being, or *shalom*, there has been a clear increase in The Groves area over the 30-plus years we have lived here. This can be inferred from obvious indicators such as lower levels of crime and vandalism and virtually no incidents of racist abuse or violence, to more subtle things like neighbours looking out for each other and relating more on the street and on doorsteps. Whatever the reasons – and there will be a number – hopefully the years of park Fun Days, improvements to the park and the creation of the Community Garden, and projects such as Residents' Car Parking have helped.

An important part of our way of working is to not always be the ones who begin projects, to the point of sometimes deliberately holding back in the hope that someone else will take the initiative or have the idea, and then to get behind them and give support.

A persistent problem on our streets is litter and fly-tipping in the alleyways, usually of household rubbish, and sometimes unwanted furniture, toys, TVs, white goods (often with the packaging of the replacement). We take any opportunity to talk about the problem and when the inevitable 'they should do something about it' (meaning the council) comment is made, suggesting that maybe we who live here could do something. One elderly neighbour got a litter-picker and would pick up litter from outside his house and on the street nearby, so he could be used as an example: 'If we all did a bit, like Mr Lawlor, then we could make our streets tidy.'

Recently a note was put through our door to ask us to join in a street tidy-up. This is a great example of the sort of thing we have hoped, prayed and prompted to see – someone having a go, and encouraging others to help. All the houses were leafleted and we went to the meeting point to find it was a couple of students who were behind the tidy-up, and ready with a supply of bin bags and plastic gloves. Besides the four of us, one other adult and about ten children joined in and a lot of litter was bagged and gathered with larger items, such as an armchair, at the end of our street for a council rubbish collection. Involvement from more long-term residents would have been better, but it was still a positive start, with a real sense of achievement as we looked at the pile of bags.

The next step involved using my good relationship with our local councillors. When I contacted the council online to ask for the rubbish to be removed, the response was to give us the date of the next scheduled collection – nearly three weeks away. I sent an email to the councillors pointing out that there would probably be a far bigger mess by then, and that those who had made the effort to gather the rubbish could be discouraged from doing it again. They have an excellent understanding of local dynamics, and an extra collection was arranged within two days. Councillor Bernard Priest commented, 'When a community responds in this way the Council should support the community's timing.'[8]

Encouraging people to take pride in and take care of their local environment is an ongoing challenge. Encouraging willingness to have a go is another. The first hurdle is a 'What's the point?' mindset grown through previous knockbacks and feelings of inadequacy, often subconsciously transmitted from previous generations.

Breaking that negative cycle and generating a sense of 'I can do that' is surely a desired fruit of building well-being, or *shalom*. Is it better to work this way, to grow a neighbourly culture of taking care of our streets, or for a summer youth mission or church based outside the area to come in and pick up our litter for us? Good intentions, yes, but arguably reinforcing the dependency culture and subtly undermining the self-esteem of the local community.[9]

Involving the churches

In writing about Carisma, I have already mentioned the considerable openness in the African-Caribbean community at the start to the churches being part of the process, even an expectation that the pastors would take a lead in forming what was to become Carisma. However, most of them did not attend community meetings. This was noticed and the audible comment by a lady at one of the meetings as she looked around the room, 'Where are the pastors?' was an expression of surprise mixed with indignation.

Such instances, together with a lack of presence at other events and meetings and little involvement by most churches in PeaceWeek, led to a probably subconscious, but nevertheless discernible, change in community attitude. Whereas in the early days church leaders were invited to meetings and events as a matter of course, years of inconsistency in turning up had a cumulative effect of them *not* tending to come to mind when invitation lists were made. For instance, the community members invited to meet with then Prime Minister Tony Blair in February 2007 did not include any church or faith-group leaders –

not through any deliberate act or intention that I am aware of – it just did not occur to anyone.[10]

A seeming unwillingness by comparatively well-organised churches to adapt to the community's often last-minute way of doing things was noticeable. As an example, after a young man was shot and killed in the nearby Hulme area,[11] members of Carisma picked up on a desire in the community to do something to mark this tragedy in some way. With help from Mothers Against Violence and the local Street Pastors, a candlelit march to the scene of the shooting and vigil was hastily organised for the Sunday evening, and through some rapid dissemination by phone, email and word of mouth, a good number of people came, including the local MP Tony Lloyd and several councillors.[12]

Out of a number of local church leaders contacted, the response from the few we heard back from was that their Sunday evening services were organised and could not be cancelled, or – as was suggested – relocated. So, apart from a few individual congregation members, once again the absence of local churches and their leaders was glaring, and once again it was noticed. 'What are they doing that's more important than this?' was one comment I recall.

Of course, church services need to be arranged in advance, but grieving local people will not appreciate that as an excuse. Presumably the short notice was also problematic for the MP and councillors who attended. I would still maintain that, with a bit of imagination and effort, the churches could at least have organised for some representatives to be there.

PeaceWeek, with the same positive ethos as Carisma, and the addition of a sharp focus and high-profile activity, seemed to me to be an even clearer example of seeking to build *shalom* in our community (and therefore 'mission-with' 'project-praxis' for Christians participating). Surely those churches who seemed reticent about supporting Carisma would now get on board, even if it was to have a peace-themed Sunday service during PeaceWeek – something they would be in control of? There was a lot of biblical material to draw on. However, the levels of recognition, support and encouragement given by council officers, councillors and police were, for the most part, not matched by the churches. To find out more about the reasons behind the wide variation in involvement by local churches I conducted a series of interviews with church leaders in 2010.[13]

One of the responses I received when asking about PeaceWeek, particularly from evangelical church leaders, was that they could not get involved because they had their own programme of events running that week, or sometimes simply that it was not a priority for them over what they normally do. A few more conservative churches had issues working with other churches. This suggests a theological prioritising based on a narrower view of mission. There was also a correlation between lesser likelihood of involvement in PeaceWeek and a lower proportion of local people in a congregation which raises 'mission-with'-related questions about how much the church identified with the area, or had been affected by members moving away to other areas.[14]

This same theological prioritising was also seen in the reaction when I was invited to speak about PeaceWeek to a group of evangelical leaders from a much wider area at a Manchester planning meeting for a year-long national campaign called HOPE08.[15] I presented it as an opportunity to work in a different way, *with* the local community, and suggested partnering with churches across the city as a part of the social action aspect of HOPE08. Maybe it was coincidental, but several chose this late item on the agenda as the moment to leave the meeting. I was given a polite hearing by the rest, but no one responded.

These disappointing responses to a viable community-led initiative on an issue of shared concern – a rarity in inner-city areas – has a bearing on 'mission-with' in terms of how local churches tend to see their mission and priorities which would appear to more 'mission-for' and 'mission-to'. These are less dependent on having a strong and consistent local presence.

Another example of church leaders, particularly evangelicals, not 'getting' this 'with' aspect of mission, or, more likely, prioritising other aspects, concerns Community Organising. Several years ago a number of Christians (including myself), together with people of other faiths, were involved in setting up a Manchester Community Organising body, known as 'ChangeMakers', to campaign on issues of injustice. When I invited a group of evangelical leaders to an early meeting to formulate policies and strategies, only two came. They looked uncomfortable, made no contributions beyond introducing themselves along with everyone else present, and did not come again. In conversation later both said politely that they thought it was a great thing, but they did not feel personally that it was a priority for them.

It's not all negative, however. While there was no specific church support asked for or given to the Residents' Car Parking campaign, several churches, to varying degrees, have given support to the park Fun Days and our small events in the Community Garden. This has ranged from the free loan of chairs and tables, and a minibus to move them, to a local vicar now being a fixture as the Fun Day DJ, and church members attending events. This involvement has raised the credibility of those churches with local people, helping to lower any us/them barriers, and has actually resulted in people attending Carol Services and accessing other activities run by local churches or in their buildings such as youth clubs, toddler groups and job clubs.

It is the same story with those churches who did get involved more fully with PeaceWeek, not just in terms of credibility with the community as solidarity was shown with an issue that concerned them, but also in noting a positive effect on the congregation, something several leaders in my survey spoke of:

> In terms of our commitment to the community, to be seen as a place where we proclaim peace is quite significant. It not only gives a good message to the wider community of Manchester, but it also gives people a focus for their own need to be doing something. They like to feel that there's something they can be involved in that is actually going to make a difference.

This feeling of general improvement in well-being is hard to quantify, but I would be curious to know if the programmes and priorities of some of those other churches who chose not to get involved had comparable results.

---

[1] Steve Chalke. Quote from 'Faith in Politics,' Christian Socialist Movement Conference 2001.

[2] However, it should be noted that though young black men were in the majority, the widespread perception of the gangs as being a 'black problem' does not hold up at the very basic level of their mixed ethnic composition. This perception also hides the true basis of gang participation as shared economic and social marginalisation, rather than ethnic solidarity. 'However, although ethnicity was a shaping force in local street cultures, it is clear that the violent youth gang phenomenon is not reducible to a question of race. ... Indeed, in seeking an explanation of the gang phenomenon, we have found that social class offers a more salient explanatory schema than race.' John Pitts, *Reluctant Gangsters: The Changing Face of Youth Crime* (Cullompton, Devon: Willan, 2008) p.5. One study estimated 25 per cent of gang-involved young people in Manchester were white and 10 per cent Asian. S. Shropshire, & M. McFarquhar, *Developing Multi Agency Strategies to Address the Street Gang Culture and Reduce Gun Violence Amongst Young People* (Manchester: Steve Shropshire & Michael McFarquhar Consultancy Group, September 2002) p.5. Another identified the make-up of the Gooch gang (Moss Side) as 70 per cent mixed race, 10 per cent white, 20 per cent other; Doddington

(Moss Side) 60 per cent mixed race/African-Caribbean, 40 per cent white; Longsight Crew 70 per cent mixed race/African-Caribbean, 15 per cent Asian, 10 per cent white, 5 per cent other; Longsight Soldiers 50 per cent mixed race, 50 per cent white. C. P. Coughlan, *A Study to detect the magnitude of the youth crime problem in the North West of England*. A dissertation submitted to the University of Manchester for the degree of MRes in the Faculty of Social Sciences and Law, 2003, p.41.

[3] Gustavo Gutiérrez, *The Power of the Poor in History* (Maryknoll, NY: Orbis 1983) p.17.

[4] Hebrews 4:15.

[5] While speaking from a Christian standpoint, I recognise that Christians do not have a monopoly on such views.

[6] Romans 12:18 (NCV).

[7] Lovell, *Church and Community Development*, pp.37–38.

[8] Email, 2nd August 2016.

[9] Another example of supporting someone else's idea involved the bumper crop from the plum tree in the Community Garden this summer. One of our neighbours offered to make lots of plum jam to give out to everyone who came to the Bring and Share event, so we helped bring in the harvest!

[10] 'To tell the truth when I think back at that time … the church leaders did not spring to mind as they were not the ones in the forefront making things happen and trying to make a difference with regards to young people and violent street crime.' Email from Erinma Bell, 15th June 2009.

[11] *Manchester Evening News*, 15th September 2005, http://www.manchestereveningnews.co.uk/news/greater-manchester-news/teenage-dad-shot-on-eve-of-birthday-1084481 (accessed 5th October 2016).

[12] The vigil took place on Sunday, 18th September 2005, http://www.manchestereveningnews.co.uk/news/greater-manchester-news/peace-march-after-murder-1084852 (accessed 5th October 2016).

[13] This survey of leaders of 24 churches in the area formed part of the research for an MPhil degree.

[14] A phenomenon identified by Church Growth analysts as 'Redemption and Lift'. More on this in Part 4 below.

[15] 'HOPE08 sought to catalyse, encourage and support churches across the UK as, through words and actions, they worked together and with public bodies such as government, police and the media in service to their communities.' Theos, *The Whole Church, for the Whole Nation, for the Whole Year: An Evaluation of HOPE08* (London: Theos, 2009) p.14.
http://www.hopetogether.org.uk/Publisher/File.aspx?ID=35144 (accessed 11th October 2016).

Part Four

The Wider Context

This fourth part is in two main sections. The first looks at the wider issue of the lack of Christians living in the inner city. In the second I will compare and contrast 'mission-with' to a number of other expressions of mission.

Where are we? The location of Christians

'Milligan, what are you standing there for?'
'Everybody's got to be somewhere, sir.'[1]

Our sense of calling to live where we have been living lies behind our decision to relocate as incomers, which in turn forms the context in which 'mission-with' has grown. You will probably have noticed by now a number of references to the struggles of the church in the inner city and the lack of Christians living there. Moving into the inner city was partly about, in a small way, offsetting that lack. In this section I will examine the issue of where Christians live, how those choices are made, and the resulting drift to the suburbs, beginning with a more detailed look at the theology of Martin Gooder.

Brunswick via China

It was when I started coming to Brunswick Church after I arrived in Manchester that I began learning about inner-city mission and ministry – theory and practice – through then Brunswick minister Martin Gooder. This was to prove influential in my decision to remain in the inner city, and therefore one of the foundations of what would become 'mission-with'.

Martin describes his and Carol's early thinking as based on incarnational theology and overseas missionary models, partly as they originally thought they may be going to China. They were deeply impressed by the life of Hudson Taylor who, when he first went to China, came across other English missionaries living a separated colonial lifestyle from which they shared a gospel that was confused with Western values. For Taylor this was not the gospel at all.

Effective mission required more than making forays from the safety of ex-pat enclaves and so Taylor risked ridicule for behaviour not befitting an English Victorian gentleman, such as wearing Chinese clothing. But 'it was the Chinese he wanted to win – rather than sacrifice their approval for that of the small foreign community in the Ports'.[2] He clearly had the Incarnation in mind in his justification for taking on Chinese clothing and culture, writing that as Jesus was sent to the Jews 'it became Him in all things to be like unto His brethren. In language, in costume, in everything unsinful, He made Himself one with those He sought to benefit'.[3] He goes on to write that the chief objection Chinese people had to Christianity was 'that it is a *foreign* religion, and that its tendencies are to approximate believers to foreign nations'.[4] He asserted that this had 'largely hindered the rapid dissemination of the truth among the Chinese'. Instead his practice was to 'live in their houses, making no unnecessary alterations in external form, and only so far modifying their internal arrangements as attention to health and efficiency for work absolutely require. Our present experience is proving the advantage of this course'.[5]

When their missionary calling clarified towards the inner city in England, the Gooders realised a lot of what they had learned about overseas mission applied equally to that context where there were very few Christians and little knowledge of the gospel.

They made a commitment to live in Brunswick as an expression of incarnational ministry, following the example of Hudson Taylor.

> We must be prepared to follow Jesus in the principle of the Incarnation ... by ceasing to be 'one of them' and becoming 'one of us'. There must be at least a heart-identification with the people of Brunswick, so that we share their pain, their struggles, their frustrations, their conflicts. That is why, for us, it has been essential to live in Brunswick, and for our children to grow up through the same school system as everybody else.[6]

All of this was based on a theology of Christian discipleship as total commitment to Christ, which would necessarily involve sacrifice. 'Saved to Serve' was a phrase Martin often used. This was the basis of the challenge that would be given to those who sought to join Brunswick Church – to identify with the people by living with them as the rectory family did.

The grounds for this method of ministry were in cross-cultural missionary principles and incarnational theology. 'The gospel needs to be brought from a foreign culture, and needs to be incarnated into the indigenous culture.'[7] It was possible for those from a different background to live in the inner city through having a 'missionary' attitude to life. A missionary calling involved leaving one cultural background and going to live in another, following the example of Jesus.

As with Hudson Taylor in China, the perception of the Church they found among local people was that it was foreign – for the rich. This was a characteristic of the history of the Anglican Church in the inner city[8] and so 'the Church of England in the inner city ... has never really been a church for the local people'.[9]

> The nineteenth century church allowed itself to be captured by the prevailing class structure. The upper and middle classes ruled and administered there just as they did everywhere. The lower classes were tolerated, smiled upon, and seen as worthy targets for the charitable. A truly working class style of worship, church life, leadership and evangelism was never really allowed to develop. This poses some critical questions about the church today. A middle class church is irrelevant to working class people.[10]

This view over the years has come to form part of the working-class psyche. 'A tradition had been established, and strongly reinforced by time, that the working-classes did not go to church.'[11] This was a barrier that had to be broken down and replaced with a positive alternative.

Gooder was clearly advocating what I would now identify as 'presence-among', the first stage of 'mission-with'. He was keen to see members of the church living in the local community, not as part of a missional community or in an official capacity or to enable them to do a specific project, but simply as residents and witnesses to their faith. However, as an evangelical, in terms of mission praxis, at the time his was a 'mission-to' and 'mission-for' model, with 'to' as the priority, echoing Packer's 'two tasks'.[12] Where Gooder goes beyond Packer is in his addition of sacrificial incarnational identification as a vital aspect of mission.

Redemption and lift... or leave

As the Church always operates within a host culture, there will always be an influence, and there is an ongoing task to recognise what is biblical and what is cultural. But can that influence be so seductive as to get to the point where some of its diluting effects on priorities and behaviour seem to be largely unnoticed? A strong aspect of the prevalent contemporary middle-class culture is the ambition to improve economically and socially. When alloyed with Christian discipleship, the result is a movement away from certain locations and communities and towards others, mirroring that of the wider aspirational culture. I believe this has created a physical distance between a majority of Christians – who are middle class – and a majority of the population – who are not.

There is also a cultural distance created, resulting in a mismatch between Church and many people, and much mission praxis becoming an episodic, programmed activity which requires little or no close engagement with, or appreciation of, the culture of the other. This physical and cultural distancing weakens an identificational 'presence-among' in inner-city, working-class areas, with an ensuing damaging effect on 'mission-with' praxis in those places and among those people.

In many inner-city areas and outer overspill estates the situation is critical. A report to the Church of England General Synod in 2016 by an Evangelism Task Group said decline in such areas, where attendance was already half of the national average, was more than three times as fast.[13]

Those like myself who came to Brunswick Church from beyond the estate were challenged to move in. But Martin Gooder also asked local people who had become Christians to show commitment to their community by not moving out. He recognised a process which has been identified by Church Growth experts as 'Redemption and Lift':[14]

> The well-known phenomenon of 'redemption and lift' – the acquisition of new values by new Christians leading to a move up the social scale – is as common as ever, and accelerates the process in which those with the most social energy leave the community. The place thus inevitably becomes a kind of sink for all those without the ability to succeed in life.[15]

Vincent described this process as a 'social escalator':

> Get on it poor, you get off it rich. Get on it simple, you get off it qualified. Get on it working-class, you get off it middle-class. People from small inner-city working-class churches on street corners have got on and got out. They took their churches with them, and Christianity is strong now ... in suburbia rather than the inner areas.[16]

Gooder was also aware of the frequent consequence that those previously unable to leave the area become able to leave and, invariably, did just that. He was critical of the 'selfish' Christianity he felt it indicated:

> Some inner-city churches complain that conversion encourages people to climb the social ladder and actually move out of the area – to buy their own homes. This is very draining on the inner-city churches concerned – a strong church can never be built because people move out as soon as they are converted. That is a mark of selfish Christianity and is defective – they recognise that they are saved – but not that they are <u>saved to serve</u>. Christ surely sets people free so that they can win their friends for Him. The new Christian needs an immediate missionary commitment.[17]

An important further distinction can be made between 'Redemption and Lift' and what Derek Purnell has identified and called 'Redemption and Leave'. This is something that inner-city churches often fail to recognise as a separate issue, assuming it to be a part of the 'lift' phenomenon. Purnell accepts that the 'redemption and lift' principle is 'inevitable in certain circumstances but it should not equate to "redemption and leave"'.[18] This process results in churches which are smaller or have a sizeable percentage of members travelling back in from outside the area.

Taking this further, if 'lift' is defined more tightly as the acquisition of new values, leading to positive changes in lifestyle, priorities and attitudes – which should surely be seen as fruits of conversion – and physically moving up and away is removed as an inevitable consequence, then 'Redemption and Stay' becomes an option. Vincent, in writing about the incomer's 'journey downward' and noting it is for 'those who have', allows for the kingdom bringing things like education and money to 'those who have not':

> The journey downward is for people who are doing well, who have raised themselves, who have acquired things, or people, or education, or money, or status. Jesus called them the rich, 'those who have'. But this is not addressed to 'those who have not', for whom rightly the Kingdom brings some of these things.[19]

However, the fact that this 'lift' usually does lead to 'leave' calls into question the nature of the values being taught to new Christians, and which parts of the prevailing culture are questioned and which assumed. In the survey of 24 local churches I conducted in 2010, most had seen people move away from the local area. Though the survey was intended to find out more about local church responses to PeaceWeek, these findings came about through asking about the make-up of congregations between local, ex-local and incomer. Typical answers included: 'people are moving up the social ladder, buying houses'; 'they started here and they just sort of moved out'; 'those with get up and go, get up and do just that'. This seemed to be accepted as a fact of inner-city church life with little evidence of any questioning of the phenomenon.[20]

In a middle-class dominated church there appears to be an assimilation of the aspiration to upward mobility, where the ambition is to rise as far as our economic potential and education will take us. Consequently, a promotion and boost in salary and the car or holiday it makes possible are conveniently seen as blessings from God. When local people become Christians this is imbibed as part of the prevailing culture. So when, as a consequence of their conversion, more of their potential is realised and they do more training or become capable of holding down a job or getting a better-paid one, and acquire the ability to move up and out, that is exactly what they do, as 'lift' leads to 'leave'. While the reasons for leaving may be understandable, prayerful consideration of a sense of calling to the place or community as a reason to stay, is usually not a part of the decision-making process.

Another factor is what gets modelled to local members by their church leader. If he or she is not teaching about 'where you live', is from a middle-class background, perhaps living in a separated rectory or manse, and moves on after a few years to a church in a suburban area, then some 'Redemption and Leave' in a congregation should not come as a surprise. A 2011 study of Methodist ministers showed six per cent living in the bottom fifth of most deprived postcodes.[21] A report by the *Church Times* in 2014 showed far longer vacancy times and far fewer applicants for Anglican churches in the north and in inner-city or housing estate parishes.[22]

Of the 21 local church leaders interviewed in my survey, nine lived in the areas where their churches met. In cases, however, where this is in separate rectories, vicarages or manses, some of which are further segregated by walls, gates and driveways, it is questionable to what extent this is actually 'in' the local community.

Life decision number one

It needs to be said in the defence of those who choose to move away that wanting a better experience and access to more opportunities for your children is not a bad thing in itself.[23] 'There is nothing wrong with having more money and concern for the kids – but this should not automatically equate a move.'[24] The same factors come into play for moves in the other direction. This church leader, feeling called to an inner-city parish, describes his struggle with 'downward mobility':

> I discovered how tenacious were my expectations that, as life went on, I would better my living conditions – go upwards, get richer and 'live bigger' – ideas utterly foreign to Christ's teaching. I justified them because of my family – 'it would not be fair on my children for them to suffer' (by which I meant that they might not have the same materialistic excess as their contemporaries). I little realised how much we suffer if, in fact, we have too much.[25]

Martin Gooder's point is about what, or rather who, has prior claim.

The concepts of 'saved to serve' and readiness to sacrifice, as integral to Christian discipleship for Gooder, obviously included where to live and what to do. His encouragement to Christians was 'to get their priorities right by first finding a church where they could belong and choosing their new areas on that basis'.[26] Finding a job and/or home and then looking for a church would be the wrong way round. This reversal of the usual order of things is an echo of Jesus' challenge to His disciples and those who wish to be His disciples – if you want to be first, be the last; to be the greatest, become the least; to gain life, lose it.[27] It explains the calling of Brunswick members to move in or stay near the church, and challenging the 'Redemption and Lift/Leave' tendency, a link also made by Purnell writing about people moving out:

> In our discipleship generally we accept a capitalist and unbiblical ideal that our career is the most important factor and where we live and worship works out from that. We do this rather than recognising that *every believer* has a call on their life and needs to discover how and where God wants us to serve Him in this world. Our career should then serve that principle rather than dictate to it.[28]

He then adds that the church should reciprocate by supporting its members in their workplaces and not just see them as resources for church activities. This is a strong theme of the work of Mark Greene and the London Institute of Contemporary Christianity.

Tom Sine also wonders if as the Church we 'have allowed modernity and Western culture instead of biblical faith to shape the aspirations and values that drive our lives'[29] and asserts that:

life decision number one for followers of Jesus ... is discovering how God wants to use our lives to be a part of God's loving conspiracy. Then we make all the other important life decisions – where to work, where to live and even whom to marry – in light of that first decision.[30]

Sine goes on to say, with Purnell, that Christian calling is for all, and not an elitist notion or just for so-called 'full-time workers' such as pastors and missionaries. One of the most important responsibilities of the local church is to help its members 'discern our calling, write it down, and begin to orchestrate our entire lives around our sense of God's call, just as Jesus did'.[31] For a decision as major as choosing or changing where we live there will be a number of factors to consider, many of them positives. Surely, for a Christian, consideration of calling needs to be one of them.

Cultural blindness

Writing from a Roman Catholic perspective, Richard Rohr criticises a cultural blindness and compliance with prevailing culture in the Church, resulting in a Christianity which has failed to discern wider cultural impact and 'has not succeeded in naming the real evils well' that are destroying Western society.[32] For him, most Christian ministry is concerned with '"churching" people into symbolic, restful, and usually ethnic belonging systems rather than any real spiritual transformation into the mystery of God'.[33]

He goes on to quote Thomas Merton, writing of believers whose faith practice becomes habitual and peripheral leading to lives which are 'essentially the same as the lives of their materialistic neighbors whose horizons are purely those of the world and its transient values'.[34]

For Walter Brueggemann, 'discipleship requires a whole new conversation in a church that has been too long accommodationist and at ease in the dominant values of culture that fly in the face of the purposes of God'.[35]

Alan Roxburgh identifies individualism as one of these dominant values which has eclipsed *shalom*-based kingdom principles of relational mutual accountability and responsibility to the extent that people 'choose to go away from their neighbourhoods to join worshipping groups that suit their tastes and match their demographics'. This individualism is also seen 'in the ways we move wherever we might want to find work that maximises our personal goals'.[36]

Ann Morisy also sees a dangerous entanglement with the mainstream: 'So far the Church has found it more acceptable to speak up on behalf of the poor than to confront the mainstream culture which forms us so extensively.'[37] She wonders if our diffidence about the 'dishonesty and denial that infect suburban and affluent living' is because 'challenging "the mainstream" risks biting the hand that feeds us, and risks onlookers inspecting our lifestyle and wagging their heads as they find it no different than their own'.[38] Ironically, this is at a time of hunger in society for 'transformative experiences', as people reach saturation point with acquiring stuff – something already being exploited in advertising by associating products with experiences rather than what they can actually do. This represents an opportunity for the

Church as 'the original purveyor of transformative experiences'.[39]

If, as Sine states, we have in the Western Church a view of conversion limited to transformation of the spiritual and moral, asking how we are influenced by the values of the dominant culture is something that will rarely, if ever, happen (let alone appear as a subject for Sunday morning teaching).[40] If the Church is accommodating aspects of modern culture uncritically, to the point that 'Religious Activities' are included among lists of hobbies on consumer surveys, then there is a serious issue.

Distance

Being a 'presence-among' is an essential prerequisite for 'mission-with' praxis. How effectively can a church or individual Christian minister practise mission from a physical and cultural distance without trying to overcome the divide? Such mission praxis has a real danger of being seen as reaching in to make 'them' like 'us',[41] and of making new Christians with an inbuilt aspiration to assume the culture of their mentors rather than grow in faith within their own. There is a desire to see others becoming fellow Christians, as that is one of the goals of mission (though it must be filtered through the Great Commandment), but how can that be separated from also becoming middle-class suburban? David Sheppard in the classic *Built as a City* stated that:

> Christian behaviour is confused with middle-class behaviour ... Once a working-class man takes up middle-class behaviour patterns, he is a major step

nearer emigrating either mentally or physically from the social grouping in which he has grown up and the district in which he lives.[42]

Is there an assumption of the superiority of a certain lifestyle and culture, which happens to be the one we own? Bosch speaks of a time when Western Christians 'were unconscious of the fact that their theology was culturally conditioned; they simply assumed that it was supracultural and universally valid'.[43]

Laurie Green states that this methodology of the old missionaries is still a danger to be aware of: 'It is all too easy to enter into a deprived area or culture ... expecting to introduce God into the place of mission and in fact introducing only an alien, gentrified culture.'[44]

The effect should be not to pull individuals out of their culture or context but to permit them to become authentic followers of Jesus within it. Thus, 'incarnational mission means that people will get to experience Jesus on the inside of their culture's meaning systems.'[45] Stott comments that conversion 'does not require the convert to step right out of his former culture into a Christian sub-culture which is totally distinctive.'[46] Perhaps 'should not require' would be more accurate. This may be the ideal, but in practice is difficult to achieve.

To bring us to a place where priorities, cultural blindness and distance can be addressed and 'Redemption and Leave' can be challenged by the call to follow Jesus and its implications, we now turn to look at a biblical basis for mission as praxis arising from 'presence-among' through looking at incarnation, the call of the first disciples and the praxis of the early Church.

[1] Spike Milligan, *Adolf Hitler, My Part in his Downfall* (London, Penguin 2012), p.35.

[2] Dr and Mrs Howard Taylor, *Hudson Taylor's Spiritual Secret* (Chicago: Moody, 1932) p.28.

[3] Taylor, *China's Spiritual Needs and Claims*, p.32.

[4] Taylor, *China's Spiritual Needs and Claims*, p.32.

[5] Taylor, *China's Spiritual Needs and Claims*, p.32.

[6] Gooder, *Brunswick Papers*, p.20. Several of their contemporaries in inner-city parishes for various reasons lived further out and travelled in.

[7] Gooder, *Brunswick Papers*, p.30.

[8] 'The Church of England has never enjoyed a golden age in urban Britain'. Archbishop of Canterbury's Commission on Urban Priority Areas, *Faith in the City* (London: Church House Publishing, 1985) pp.45–46.

[9] Interview with Martin and Carol Gooder, 25th November 2010. While this, as stated in *Faith in the City*, can be argued in an institutional sense, there have been a good number of individual congregations, such as Brunswick, that have worked hard to identify with inner-city communities.

[10] Robin Gamble, *The Irrelevant Church* (Tunbridge Wells: Monarch, 1991) p.63.

[11] Gamble, *Irrelevant Church*, p.36. In the early eighties Joslin estimated church-going in working-class areas at less than one per cent. Roy Joslin, *Urban Harvest: Biblical perspectives on Christian mission in the inner cities* (Welwyn: Evangelical Press, 1982) p.46. Given the overall decline since, that figure is unlikely to have improved.

[12] 'Meeting the social needs of man is important, but it is not the gospel.' Gooder, *Brunswick Papers*, p.103 (his underlining). There was a similar view in black-led evangelical churches: a pastor once said to me that his priority was to preach the

gospel: a fireman might occasionally use his ladder to rescue a stranded cat, but not to the detriment of his main job which was to put out fires.

[13] Report from the Archbishops' Evangelism Task Group, p.15, https://www.churchofengland.org/media/2442380/gs_2015_-_evangelism_tg_report.pdf (accessed 5th October 2016). Also reported in *The Times*: 'Church "abandons council estates" for richer parishes', http://www.thetimes.co.uk/tto/faith/article4692 300.ece?shareToken=0db768846e41edc98918ecda4dacd91f (accessed 5th October 2016).

[14] The term first appeared in Donald McGavran, *The Bridges of God: A Study in the Strategy of Missions* (London: World Dominion Press, 1955).

[15] Tony Adamson, *Inner City Evangelism – A Personal Reflection* (Nottingham: Grove 1993) p.7.

[16] John Vincent, *Into the City* (London: Epworth, 1982) p.112.

[17] Gooder, *Brunswick Papers*, p.170 (his underlining).

[18] Derek Purnell, 'Urban Presence,' in John Vincent, ed., *Faithfulness in the City* (Hawarden: Monad, 2003) p.69.

[19] Vincent, *Radical Jesus*, p.83.

[20] Back when he was at Brunswick, Martin Gooder would personally challenge those he became aware of who were considering moving away. Unique in my experience! 'I had to say fairly strongly to the people who became Christians, listen, I live here and I'm committed to stay here. Some of our Christians … have made big sacrifices to move in. What gives you the right, now you're doing well because you're Christians, to move out? And I think it hit them between the eyes, that this is what made the church, this was how they became Christians and therefore if they were serious about following Christ, they too need to stay put for the sake of the church.' Interview with Martin and Carol Gooder.

[21] Michael Hirst, 'Location, Location, Location', *Methodist Recorder*, 10th May 2012, p.8.

[22] Madelaine Davies, 'Clergy flock to fill posts in "wealthy" south-east', *Church Times*, 7th February 2014, http://www.churchtimes.co.uk/articles/2014/7-february/news/uk/clergy-flock-to-fill-posts-in-wealthy-south-east (accessed 5th October 2016). 'When the Revd Philip North's former parish on a large Hartlepool estate fell vacant recently, it was two-and-a-half years before the diocese could find anyone to fill the post. "Compare that with a recent vacancy in a richly endowed parish near Paddington, which attracted 123 firm applicants, and you will see the true measure of the spiritual health of the Church of England," he told the General Synod in November.'

[23] In some cases, such as where addiction is an issue, getting a fresh start away from a context of temptation is actually necessary.

[24] Purnell, 'Urban Presence', p.69.

[25] Charlie Cleverly, *Epiphanies of the Ordinary: Encounters that change lives* (London: Hodder & Stoughton, 2012) p.163.

[26] Gooder, *Brunswick Papers*, p.9.

[27] Mark 8:34-37; 9:35; 10:42-45.

[28] Purnell, 'Urban Presence', p.69.

[29] Tom Sine, 'The Wrong Dream,' *Tear Times*, Autumn 1996.

[30] Tom Sine, *The New Conspirators: Creating the Future One Mustard Seed at a Time* (Bletchley: Paternoster, 2008) p.236.

[31] Sine, *New Conspirators*, p.236.

[32] Richard Rohr and Andreas Ebert, *The Enneagram: A Christian Perspective* (Campbell, CA: Crossroads, 2002) p.xvi.

[33] Rohr and Ebert, *The Enneagram*, p.xvi.

[34] Thomas Merton, *Living Bread* (New York: Farrar, Straus & Cudahy, 1956) p.xxii.

[35] Walter Brueggemann, *The Word That Redescribes the World: The Bible and Discipleship* (Minneapolis: Fortress, 2006) p.95.

[36] Alan Roxburgh, 'Reclaiming the Commons: What it is and why it is important', *Journal of Missional Practice*, Spring 2016.

http://journalofmissionalpractice.com/reclaiming-the-commons (accessed 6th October 2016). Roxburgh defines 'God's dream' as 'the shared life and the place where that dream is turned into reality is the local'.

[37] Ann Morisy, *Journeying Out: A New Approach to Christian Mission* (London: Morehouse, 2004) p.96.

[38] Morisy, *Journeying Out*, p.96.

[39] Morisy, *Journeying Out*, p.219.

[40] Sine, *New Conspirators*, p.77. 'Too many of us have been conditioned to unconsciously baptize those values instead of question them.'

[41] 'The mission on the margins is not to bring the margins into the centre, which always means that the centre dominates the margins, and either co-opts or excommunicates its members. The mission on the margins is intended to constantly challenge the centre with viable, relevant alternatives, so that the centre can itself be part of the margins.' John Vincent, 'Basics of Radical Methodism', in Joerg Rieger and John J. Vincent, *Methodist and Radical: Rejuvenating a Tradition* (Nashville: Kingswood, 2003) p.46.

[42] David Sheppard, *Built as a City* (London: Hodder & Stoughton 1974) pp.60–61.

[43] Bosch, *Transforming Mission*, p.448. 'Mission in the colonial era had a very thick Western accent.' Stan Nussbaum, *A Reader's Guide to Transforming Mission* (Maryknoll, NY: Orbis, 2005) pp.107.

[44] Green, 'I Can't Go *There*!', p.5.

[45] Michael Frost and Alan Hirsch, *The Shaping of Things to Come* (Peabody, MA: Hendrickson, 2003) p.40. Frost and Hirsch are strong on reaching people within their own cultures, but emphasise using work and leisure networks, which is more fitting for a dormitory town than an inner-city context.

[46] John Stott, *Christian Mission in the Modern World* (London: Falcon, 1975) p.122.

Incarnation, following and fascination

Incarnation

The climactic act in God's mission – the *missio Dei* – to estranged humankind was to become one of us. Jesus was the embodiment of a human life lived in union with the Creator and Father God – the ultimate incomer. Not only 'man', but also 'a man', 'born in a particular place at a particular time'[1] and within a particular host culture: the '200-percent person'.[2] This close identification with those He came to can be seen as the definitive expression of 'presence-among'.[3] 'The Word became flesh and made his dwelling among us.'[4]

The title given to Jesus of 'Emmanuel', meaning 'God with us', sums it up and points to the 'with' aspect of mission. No wonder 'with' has been called 'the most important word in theology'.[5]

Missionally, then, incarnation is about going, or being sent, to a people group, making our dwelling among them, and embodying the host culture, rather than issuing an invitation for them to come to us.[6] Jesus' commissioning of His disciples, according to John's Gospel: 'As the Father sent me, I now send you',[7] shows continuity with His mission.

Vincent calls incarnation the 'decisive gift of Christianity ... not just the gift of incarnation in Jesus, but the gift of constant incarnations'.[8] Bosch describes the Christian faith as 'intrinsically incarnational ... as the church will always enter into the context in which it happens to find itself'.[9]

Davey writes, 'if God became human, the experiences and concerns of being human are those of the divine.'[10] Incarnation 'is as much about faithfulness in the mundanity of everyday life as the sweep of the kingdom amidst the powers',[11] and incarnational principles are 'critical to urban mission bringing an understanding of the human dimension at the heart of the *missio Dei*, as well as the potential to discover the divine "at home" and "at work" within the urban culture and society'.[12]

In the light of this incarnational model of close and intimate identification, each follower of Jesus needs to discern their individual calling, to be sent as the Father sent Him, and the first question, given the importance of place as a focus of incarnation, should be 'Where?' Given God's 'preferential love for the poor',[13] should going to where they are be the default rather than the exception?

Following Jesus: location, vocation, relationships

Beginning with the calling of the first disciples, Jesus' words, 'Follow me,' clearly had practical implications and were not just something intellectual or spiritual.[14] Nets, boats and a tax booth were left behind, signifying preparedness to leave jobs and security – similarly family members, homes and villages – 'for the sake of the kingdom of God'.[15] Commentators agree:

> So compelling is the claim of Jesus upon them that all prior claims lose their validity. Their father, the hired servants, the boat and the nets are left behind as they commit themselves in an exclusive sense to follow Jesus.[16]

The ties were not broken in some sort of cultic isolationism as Jesus is shortly afterwards teaching and healing from Peter's home,[17] has a meal at Levi's house[18] immediately after Levi 'left everything' to follow Him, and one of the fishermen later has to catch the fish with the coin in its mouth.[19] This was about a reordering of priorities and deciding what really mattered. Location, vocation, relationships – everything was on the line for the sake of the Pearl of Great Price. Differences in context and culture notwithstanding – this was an itinerant rabbi they were being asked to accompany[20] – there was a cost to following this teacher that they were willing to pay. It is referred to on other occasions,[21] and seen by the disciples themselves as significant.[22]

In Mark, Jesus' public ministry opens with words summarising His message: 'Repent and believe the good news!'[23] Repentance, or conversion (Gk: *metanoia*), means a turning round of the whole person, inside and out, and is a call to discipleship.[24]

The challenge to anyone wishing to be a disciple to deny self and take up the cross also signifies a change of attitude and a willingness to sacrifice. Hence, Martin Gooder's mantra: 'saved to serve'.

Brueggemann traces back the call to follow given by Jesus to that made by the God of the Old Testament who calls and sends and 'disrupts the lives of settled people, who gives them a vocation which marks life by inconvenience and risk'.[25] Choosing Abraham and Moses as examples, he states that they had their lives, respectively, 'radically displaced' and 'wrenched away from what he might have thought was the circumstance of his life and radically relocated'.[26]

> The same God, in the life and in the utterances of Jesus, makes the same claim in the New Testament. In each case the call, an authorizing imperative, is a disruption that set lives on totally new trajectories that has not previously been in purview.[27]

Citing the calls to the four fishermen in Mark chapter one, and other examples of calling in Mark, he concludes that in all these cases 'it is clear that Jesus enacts a major claim upon people's lives that places their lives in crisis, the same sovereign claim that is so uncompromising in the narratives of Abraham and Moses'.[28]

In direct parallel, Brueggeman continues, despite the leap from these to our own 'times, places and circumstances', the same God today calls people into His Church. Not to join an institution but 'to sign on for a different narrative account of reality that is in profound contrast to the dominant account of reality into which we are all summarily inducted'. In describing what this entails, in terms of what we are called away from and towards, he concludes that it is indeed to an 'impossibility'.[29]

When the rich young man walked away sadly, having been told that his wealth was what came between him and the kingdom of God, and it all had to go, Jesus 'loved him' but did not go after him and try to negotiate a percentage.[30]

Perhaps in the name of being relevant and not putting people off, we are tempted to present the gospel as a mediocre tack on to the good life. But you cannot simply add the Jesus lifestyle on top of a normal, respectable lifestyle.[31]

An old hymn, still popular today, puts it like this:

Long ago apostles heard it
by the Galilean lake,
turned from home and work and family,
leaving all for his dear sake.

Jesus calls us! By your mercy,
Savior, may we hear your call,
give our hearts to your obedience,
serve and love you best of all.[32]

'Turned from home and work and family'. When we sing these words (and those of many other hymns and songs where we make 'All for Jesus'-type promises), do we realise just what it is we are committing to do?

Jesus' encouragement to His followers to 'seek first [the kingdom of God] and his righteousness, and all these things will be given to you as well' clearly shows the changes of priority and attitude that are behind a distinctive Christian lifestyle. 'These things' refers back to basics such as food and clothing, essentials which people run after and worry about. Our contrasting attitude, based on putting God's kingdom first, before our needs, is to be one of not worrying as, 'your heavenly Father knows that you need them.'[33]

Jesus does not condemn aspiration so much as turn it on its head. 'Anyone who wants to be first must be the very last, and the servant of all.'[34] It is not the seeking, but what to seek and how to attain it.

Davey lists a number of consequences in the Gospels of encountering Jesus:

> Some are called to follow, others to go home, some are called to testify, others to keep silent, some to embrace a radical break with possessions, home and family, others to rebuild relationships. To go home is not to opt out of discipleship but to live as a restored sign of the kingdom break in. While those who are called to minister may experience the need to follow Christ into another location, others will find that their discipleship lies in the familiar and the challenges of faith lived in the midst of family and neighbours in their own Galilee or Nazareth.[35]

However, this should not be seen as a list of options for the disciple to choose between. In a master/servant relationship the servant must be prepared for any of these, and more. It is the coach who decides where his players will play on the pitch. Lovell, commenting on the salt, light and yeast, all of which Jesus calls His followers to be, says that 'each element fulfils its function when placed in proper relationship to something else'.[36] As a part of that relationship, I would include proportionate distribution.

Writing about mission and reaching the entire country, Mark Greene warns of the problems caused by a 'sacred-secular divide', defined as 'the pervasive belief that some parts of life are not really important to God – work, school, sport, TV – but anything to do with prayers, church services and church-based activities is'.[37] He advocates 'whole life discipleship' as a counter, a holistic approach which is a positive step I would totally agree with. However, I have to question to what extent it includes consideration of location, when he seems content that already 'we have the people. And we have them in place.'[38]

Although this is also a reference to where Christians work and therefore 'spend most of their time' and 'have the highest number of ongoing relationships', thereby by his reckoning 'probably connected to over 90% of the population of the UK',[39] it does not take into account that most Christians live, work and socialise outside of the areas where the majority of the population is. This includes most of the long-term unemployed and those labelled 'NEETs' (Not in Education, Employment or Training). In recent years through the work of sociologists such as Charles Murray an 'under-class' has been identified which, according to Gamble, is 'usually outside the life and range of the Christian church'.[40]

Other factors also appear to be of no concern to Greene: 'Never mind that we are primarily middle class.'[41] What appears to be taken as a given is the location of each Christian, which, it is asserted, is where 'God has placed' them. This could be where they live or what their career is, or the fact that, being 'primarily middle class', their churches will also be mostly located in suburban areas.

Surely 'whole life discipleship' should include these important decisions as a modern-day equivalent of 'they left their nets and followed him'?[42] This calling of the first disciples in Mark's Gospel clearly shows a preparedness to change both location and vocation, and to leave behind family, all being made subject to the call to follow.

If all Christians are actually living – or working – where God has 'placed' them, given the proportion in the inner city, that would seem to be a massive contradiction to God's 'preference' for the poor. Can we speak of God 'placing' His people without any consideration of what factors were included or omitted in the decision to live or work in a particular location? If not, this would seem to imply that in every case where a job or promotion is offered or a house in a certain street comes on to the market it is down to the leading and blessing of God, who has guided the Christian to that place. Given that Christians are predominantly located in suburban areas, this is in fact saying that the calling of God is subject to and governed by human ambition and aspiration.

Sine puts it quite bluntly:

Many of the popular Christian teachings on discipleship are extremely narrow. They tend to limit the call to follow Jesus Christ to one small spiritual compartment of life. In all the other compartments they unquestioningly let the culture call the shots. For example, in spite of all the popular Christian teaching about Jesus' lordship, it's commonly understood what comes first. Our careers come first. Getting our house in the suburbs comes first. Our upscale lifestyles come first. Then, with whatever time, energy, or resources are left, we can follow Christ.[43]

This is a long way from what Kraybill sees as the action of the kingdom of God – presented by Jesus as a 'new order breaking in on old ways, old values, old assumptions'. It 'shatters the assumptions which govern our lives' so that we can no longer 'assume that things are right just because "that's the way they are"'.[44]

Rather than 'placed', Gittins actually uses the term 'displacement'.

Those who are appropriately disturbed by the God of righteousness inevitably find their lives reoriented, redirected, and decentred: what we may call *displaced*. The life of a true disciple is no longer centred on self but on God. Disciples' lives are a continual process of displacement because they are always trying to remain faithful to the movement of God's grace and the inspiration of God's Spirit.[45]

Vincent considers discipleship 'the only true Christianity', in which following Jesus 'in his mission to people at the bottom of so-called society' is integral.[46] For those of us who come from a relatively privileged background, openness to such a 'journey downward'[47] should be a mark of discipleship. This would involve considering a call to sacrifice some or all of the potential our background, education and social connections give us to aspire to in terms of finance, status or career, to move towards those who do not have such advantages. Not primarily so that we can bestow some sort of hand-up, but in order to be with God's preferred ones and to gain real insight into the structures of sin and injustice that benefit us and disadvantage them, dynamics which work against the *shalom* of God.

The question not being asked

A constricting of discipleship teaching to exclude the 'where' of Christian service explains why there is not only a flow away from the inner city, but also little more than a trickle in the other direction. As an issue not addressed by most local churches,[48] then it is perhaps not so much a question of disobedience as of not getting as far as being a part of the average Christian's thinking. What is the modern equivalent of 'they left their nets and followed him'? Even if it was decided that the answer to this question was that this was a sort of extreme discipleship just for a special elite, beginning with the original disciples and Paul[49] and continuing today with rare heroes who become missionaries, the evidence seems to show that, for the most part, *the question is not even being asked*.

Not that we should set a particular standard of discipleship, below which God cannot use us – we all fail and need to grow. Among the 12 sent out to heal and cast out demons were Judas, Peter, James and John, all with big issues still to come. God will use what we give Him, but this limited form of discipleship, which excludes large parts of our lives, restricts our potential as His servants. The story of Jonah starts off with him not being where God clearly wanted him to be, yet even in that situation God used him to reach the sailors on the boat he took flight on.

Evangelism by fascination

As the presence of Jesus is continued through the Church and where what Lesslie Newbigin calls the 'new reality' is seen, curiosity and questions will be the result, to the point that the missionary dialogue is 'initiated by the outsider who is drawn to ask: What is the secret of this new reality, this life of praise, of justice, and of peace?'[50] The 'new reality' has to be more than what Sine calls a 'devotional add-on' to normal life.

A personal study of Jesus' actions in Mark's Gospel showed that around half of them were in response to the initiative of others. N. T. Wright notes that half of the words Jesus spoke were in response to questions related to His actions.[51] When it comes to the missional activity of the early Church, Wright says the evidence does not suggest they were 'being first century evangelicals, with everybody busily telling their neighbours about Jesus', but that they were living differently and in a way that caused a reaction. This speaks of an effective 'presence-among'. 'When people see a community that is behaving differently they say, "Maybe I should investigate."'[52] Elsewhere Wright says that evangelism that flows out from the Church 'giving itself to works of justice (putting things to rights in the community) and works of beauty' will come as a surprise. 'You mean there is more? There is a new world and it has already begun, and it works by healing and forgiveness and new starts and fresh energy?'[53]

Bosch notes that 'References to specific cases of direct missionary involvement by the churches are rare in Paul's letters' as 'the missionary dimension of the conduct of the Pauline Christians remains implicit rather than explicit.'

Rather, the lifestyles of ordinary Christians should be exemplary and 'winsome', a 'powerful magnet that draws outsiders toward the church',[54] and adding credibility to the outreach Paul and his fellow workers were engaged in.

What we do find in the letters is encouragement to faithfulness and teaching concerning how to live and behave and relate to God and to others, both within the church and outside it. The emphasis is on relationships and everyday life, not activities.

Peter echoes Jesus' words from Matthew 5:16: 'Live such good lives that they will see the good things you do and will give glory to God on the day when Christ comes again'.[55] Other examples include: 'Do all you can to live a peaceful life ... If you do, then people who are not believers will respect you';[56] 'Always be ready to answer everyone who asks you to explain about the hope you have';[57] 'Be wise in the way you act with people who are not believers, making the most of every opportunity'[58] – a passage that goes back to 2:6; 'Do not continue living like those who do not believe'.[59] This section on behaviour goes through to 6:9. Other similar sections occur in most of the letters, such as Romans 12:1 to 15:13, Philippians 2:12-18, 4:4-9.

Crucially, Paul writes to the local believers in Thessalonica, 'You know how we *lived among you* for your sake',[60] and to the Philippians, 'Join together in following my example, brothers and sisters, and just as you have us as a model, keep your eyes on those who live as we do', and 'Whatever you have learned or received or heard from me, or seen in me – put it into practice. And the God of peace will be with you.'[61]

We also find much about sacrifice and denial of self, and having a different attitude:

> Therefore, I urge you, brothers and sisters, in view of God's mercy, to offer your bodies as a living sacrifice, holy and pleasing to God – this is your true and proper worship. Do not conform to the pattern of this world, but be transformed by the renewing of your mind. Then you will be able to test and approve what God's will is – his good, pleasing and perfect will.[62]

Also noting the lack of evangelism instruction, Alan Kreider writes about the early Church growing 'by fascination as well as by words, by its creative distinctiveness, by its radiant Jesus-likeness, by its sheer hopefulness':

> The early church was growing rapidly, but in early Christian literature there are no training programmes for evangelism and practically no admonitions to evangelism. Why? I concluded, not least through reading what early Christians themselves said, that the church before the conversion of Constantine was growing because it was living in a way that fascinated people. It spoke to their needs; it addressed their questions; and it didn't so much persuade as fascinate people into new life.[63]

This 'fascination' is echoed by Bryant Myers who addresses the contemporary issue of encountering people of different cultures, nationalities, and different faiths:

> We need to do our work and live our lives in a way
> that calls attention to the new Spirit that lives within
> us and who is changing us. We need to relate to
> people ... in ways that create a sense of wonder. We
> must seek a spirituality that makes our lives
> eloquent.[64]

This requires us to be where people are, to be observable and in daily relationship, with personal mission praxis in ordinary life flowing from our 'presence-among'. As with gaining acceptance into a new culture, as noted by Kohn, it is 'that "action" that takes place in the humdrum of everyday life'[65] which is significant. Are our numerous programmes and projects, in evangelism, and also in social action, a means of manufacturing contact that we do not have already in everyday life – a substitute for an ongoing lack of engagement with a local community? Knocking on doors with leaflets or setting up a sound system on a street for an evangelistic rally to 'get contacts' would be unnecessary if church members were already a 'presence' behind some of those doors, and engaged relationally with their neighbours. If those members were encouraged Sunday by Sunday to live as Christians through the week, doing the ordinary things, then contacts and, more importantly, relationships would already be in plentiful supply. Hopefully, and with prayer, through 'fascination', some of these would lead to interest in finding out about faith. If its members had more time to spend with their neighbours through being under less pressure to staff their church's outreach programme, would that actually result in more effective mission?

Andy Flannagan notes that the drift of Christians to the suburbs has resulted in a situation where many simply do not encounter the poor and powerless. He asks, 'Could we be the generation that doesn't have to start lots of projects and programmes to connect with and help the poor, needy and marginalised among us, but we're helping them simply because they're our neighbours?'[66]

---

[1] Gustavo Gutiérrez, *The God of Life* (London: SCM, 1991) p.84. Gutiérrez calls the birth of Jesus an 'incarnation into littleness'.

[2] Lingenfelter and Mayers, *Ministering Cross-Culturally*, p.122.

[3] In a more fundamental and general sense of God present among humankind. His lifestyle for the three years of ministry was of an itinerant teacher, not settled in any one place, although the 30 pre-ministry years in Nazareth that we know so little about were lived as ordinary life as part of a particular community.

[4] John 1:14a. Or 'The Word became flesh and blood, and moved into the neighborhood.' Eugene Peterson, *The Message: The Bible in Contemporary Language* (Colorado Springs, CO, Navpress, 2004) p.1444. 'In the light of such a dwelling, place – geography itself – took on a sacred meaning.' Frost and Hirsch, *Shaping of Things to Come*, p.36.

[5] Samuel Wells, *A Nazareth Manifesto: Being With God*, p.11.

[6] Seen by Murray and others as the way forward for mission in a post-Christendom age when the Church has moved from the centre to the margins.

[7] John 20:21 (NCV).

[8] Vincent, *Hope from the City*, p.127.

[9] Bosch, *Transforming Mission*, p.191.

[10] Andrew Davey, 'Christ in the City: The Density of Presence', in Davey, ed., *Crossover City*, p.91.

[11] Davey, 'Christ in the City', p.90.

[12] Davey, 'Christ in the City,' p.92.

[13] 'God has a preferential love for the poor not because they are necessarily better than others, morally or religiously, but simply because they are poor and living in an inhuman situation that is contrary to God's will. The ultimate basis for the privileged position of the poor is not in the poor themselves but in God.' Gustavo Gutiérrez, *On Job: God-talk and the Suffering of the Innocent* (Maryknoll, NY: Orbis, 1987) p.94.

[14] Mark 1:16-20. Painter argues that the 12 disciples were a unique group that did not include Levi (Mark 3:16-18), but nevertheless he notes that Levi too was called to follow and left his place of work (Mark 2:14). John Painter, *Mark's Gospel* (London: Routledge, 1997) pp.37, 56. This would seem to be a problem for those who claim a special case for the 12, thereby excusing anyone else from such a radical response to the call to follow (for example Meier, below). It should be noted that Painter regards Levi and Matthew in Mark, the earliest Gospel, as being two different people (pp.55–57).

[15] Luke 18:29.

[16] William L. Lane, *The Gospel of Mark* (Grand Rapids, MI: Eerdmans, 1974) p.69. Two other examples from commentators: 'These scenes impress us in two ways: on the one hand, we see the authority of Jesus, who calls men to follow him and is instantly obeyed. On the other, we are reminded of the total demands that his call to discipleship makes.' Morna D. Hooker, *The Message of Mark* (London: Epworth, 1983) p.105. 'His word lays hold on men's lives and asserts his right to their whole-hearted and total allegiance, a right that takes priority even over the claims of kinship.' C. E. B. Cranfield, *The Gospel according to St Mark* (Cambridge: University Press, 1959) p.69.

[17] Mark 1:29-34.

[18] Mark 2:14-15.

[19] Matthew 17:27.

[20] Ernest Best, *Following Jesus: Discipleship in the Gospel of Mark* (Sheffield: University of Sheffield, 1981) p.171. Best sees discipleship in this Gospel presented as 'movement after Jesus'. Referring to the calling of disciples: 'At the beginning of each incident Jesus is in motion and he says to those whom he calls "come after me" i.e. get into motion.' p.171.

[21] 'If anyone would come after me, let him deny himself …' Mark 8:34-38 (ESV).

[22] 'Then Peter spoke up, "We have left everything to follow you!"' Mark 10:28.

[23] Mark 1:15.

[24] 'In fact the predominantly intellectual understanding of *metanoia* as change of mind plays very little part in the NT. Rather the decision by the whole man to turn around is stressed. It is clear that we are concerned neither with a purely outward turning nor with a merely intellectual change of ideas.' J. Goetzmann in Colin Brown, ed., *The New International Dictionary of New Testament Theology*, Vol. 1 (Carlisle: Paternoster, 1986) p.58.

[25] Brueggemann, *Word That Redescribes the World*, p.93.

[26] Brueggemann, *Word That Redescribes the World*, pp.93–94. The Old Testament has a number of examples of the calling and ministry of servants of God involving physical relocation. For instance: Abraham, Jacob, Joseph, Moses, Jeremiah, Daniel, Nehemiah, Jonah.

[27] Brueggemann, *Word That Redescribes the World*, p.94.

[28] Brueggemann, *Word That Redescribes the World*, p.95.

[29] Brueggemann, *Word That Redescribes the World*, p.95.

[30] Mark 10:22. Rowland comments that right from the start 'Christians could not easily live with the rigorous social ethics attributed to Jesus in the Gospels', and lists a number of accommodations made in the first few centuries, though redistribution of wealth from rich to poor remained a strong characteristic until this too was compromised in the fourth and

fifth centuries. Chris Rowland, *Radical Christianity* (Oxford: Polity, 1988) p.56.

[31] Jenny and Justin Duckworth, *Against the Tide, Towards the Kingdom*, New Monastic Library (Eugene, OR: Cascade Books, 2011) p.44.

[32] 'Jesus Calls Us, O'er the Tumult' (Cecil Frances Alexander, 1818–95), verses 3 and 5 (public domain).

[33] Matthew 6:32-33.

[34] Mark 9:35. Also: 10:43-44, and gaining and losing life or the world in 8:34-37 for anyone who 'would come after me' (ESV).

[35] Davey, 'Christ in the City', p.88.

[36] Lovell, *Church and Community Development*, p.35.

[37] Mark Greene, *Imagine: How We Can Reach the UK* (London: LICC, 2003) p.14.

[38] Greene, *Imagine*, p.18.

[39] Greene, *Imagine*, 17. Even if this figure was accurate I would want to define 'connected'.

[40] Gamble, *The Irrelevant Church*, p.55.

[41] Greene, *Imagine*, p.17.

[42] Mark 1:18.

[43] Tom Sine, foreword to Kraybill, *The Upside Down Kingdom*, p.9. Elsewhere Sine speaks of 'working the Jesus stuff in round the sides' of values and lifestyle already defined by our class, income and chosen way of life, making 'Christian faith as a little devotional add-on'. Tom Sine, 'Cultural Values'. Interview at Greenbelt Festival, August 2010, http://www.youtube.com/watch ?v=CX3HWCpt51Q (accessed 6th October 2016).

[44] Kraybill, *The Upside Down Kingdom*, p.23.

[45] Anthony J. Gittins, *Called to Be Sent: Co-missioned as Disciples Today* (Liguori, Missouri: Liguori, 2008) p.14. Despite this, and describing 'missional' in terms of boundary-breaking, pushing through privilege and segregation to inclusion and welcome, with missional living something 'every professing Christian

must urgently discover and practice' (p.46), Gittins never goes into the implications of what that might mean in everyday life.

[46] Vincent, 'Losing Life, Gaining Life', in John Vincent, ed, *Mark Gospel of Action: Personal and Community Responses* (London: SPCK, 2006) p.69.

[47] Vincent, 'Losing life, Gaining Life', p.75.

[48] 'We encourage local involvement but we don't ever preach about where you live. … We wouldn't give any direction in that area.' Local church leader commenting on ex-locals and incomers from my 2010 survey.

[49] Meier, in considering the implications of following Jesus, concludes that we are led to 'the obvious insight that we 20th-century Christians can appropriate and live the New Testament arche-type of discipleship only in a partial, metaphorical, or spiritualised way'. John P. Meier, 'The Disciples of Christ: Who Were They?' in *Mid-Stream*, Vol. 38, nos. 1–2, January–April 1999, p.134.

[50] Lesslie Newbigin, *The Gospel in a Pluralist Society* (London: SPCK ,1989) p.134.

[51] N. T. Wright, 'N. T. Wright on Mission' – an interview with N. T Wright, http://www.hopetogether.org.uk/Media/PlayMedia.aspx?download=file&media_id=77115&file_id=85756 (accessed 11th October 2016).

[52] Wright, 'N. T. Wright on Mission'.

[53] N. T. Wright, *Surprised by Hope* (London: SPCK, 2007) p.244.

[54] Bosch, *Transforming Mission*, p.137.

[55] 1 Peter 2:12b, NCV.

[56] 1 Thessalonians 4:11a, 12a, NCV.

[57] 1 Peter 3:15, NCV.

[58] Colossians 4:5, NCV.

[59] Ephesians 4:17, NCV.

[60] 1 Thessalonians 1:5 (my emphasis).

[61] Philippians 3:17; 4:9. See also: 1 Corinthians 10:31 – 11:1. Thessalonians 3:8-10.

[62] Romans 12:1-2. See also: Romans 6:13; 2 Corinthians 5:15, etc; Galatians 6:24; Philippians 3:7-8.

[63] Alan Kreider, *Becoming a Peace Church* (London: HHSC Christian Press, 2000) p.36.

[64] Bryant Myers, *Walking With the Poor: Principles and Practices of Transformational Development* (Maryknoll, NY: Orbis, 2000) p.321.

[65] Kohn, 'Becoming an Islander', p.145.

[66] 'Music and Politics', Interview with Andy Flannagan, http://www.surefish.co.uk/culture/music/2012/010612-andy-flannagan-interview.html (accessed 6th October 2016).

Comparisons: 'mission-with' and other mission models

Up to now I have been examining a model of mission, centred around and developed out of my experience as a Christian incomer to a particular location. 'Mission-with' requires close connection with a community, a 'presence-among', out of which arises 'project-praxis' with and alongside others.

There are, of course, many other expressions of mission, and in this section I will briefly survey a number that contain elements of or have similarities with 'mission-with' praxis. I have mentioned some of them already. They are a mix of methods, projects and people as examples of models. The first four are to do with ways of working, the next three assume or involve local presence, and the last seven also involve relocation as an incomer. The intention is to be illustrative rather than exhaustive as the field of mission is sufficiently large for there to be, no doubt, others that I am not aware of, and there is some overlap between several of them. You may notice a rough pattern of starting furthest away from, then getting closer to, a fuller synergy with 'mission-with'.

The profusion of models of mission is evidence of much effort and energy being put in to rediscover mission for a post-Christendom age where the Church finds itself in a very different position in society, and the increasing acceptance of the wider conception of mission as *missio Dei*. It is worth repeating the words of David Bosch: 'Mission is a multi-faceted ministry in respect of witness, service, justice, healing, reconciliation, liberation, peace, evangelism, fellowship, church planting, contextualisation, and much more.'[1]

With the more generic categories of church planting or Emerging Church I have selected a specifically urban, geographical example. Some of the other examples or projects listed could also be seen, or claimed, as planting or emerging, or 'Fresh Expressions' (for example, 'missional community'), but such labelling is not really of concern here because I am looking more for elements of praxis shared with the 'mission-with' model such as partnership, building *shalom*, or 'presence-among', particularly with reference to an inner-city context.

Co-belligerence

The first model is some distance from my approach, but does involve Christians partnering with non-Christians in a limited way on a shared concern. A military term meaning to form an alliance against a common enemy, co-belligerence used in a mission context has been described as 'the activity of Christians working together with non-Christians for a common political, economic or cultural cause'.[2] It was advocated by Francis Schaeffer as an alternative for evangelicals to the extremes of separatism or compromised alliance:

A co-belligerent is a person with whom I do not agree on all sorts of vital issues, but who, for

whatever reasons of their own, is on the same side
in a fight for some specific issue of public justice.[3]

Examples include campaigns on Sunday trading, free speech, assisted suicide and human trafficking, and indeed could encompass any issue-based initiative or project raising awareness of an injustice that resonates with a Christian mandate to be agents of *shalom*.[4] So, a working 'with', but in a limited way as a marriage of convenience, as it were. Langlois calls it a 'dangerous business',[5] sharing with Strange a strong degree of caution and mistrust of the other party or parties, and little regard for building relationship beyond the issue at hand. While I acknowledge a 'with' element here, it seems to be a reluctant, risk-free partnership to achieve a predetermined Christian moral aim, where care is taken to retain control. There could even be a hint of arrogance based on a view of the Christian partner as superior and setting the agenda. There is no notion of 'presence-among', the first part of 'mission-with'.

Make Poverty History

This is an example of Christians working with others in partnership on a shared concern on a global scale. It could be compared to the co-belligerence model only in that it is also a coming together on an issue. The inequality, caution and mistrust characteristic of the latter are absent here – perhaps because resolving the issue was seen as more important than who held the reins or got the credit. It was formed in 2005 as the UK expression of a worldwide Global Call to Action Against Poverty, and its high-profile campaign was at the G8 Summit in Edinburgh in July 2007. The movement grew out of the Christian-initiated Jubilee 2000 coalition (now Jubilee Debt Campaign UK) which, from playing a leading role in putting Make Poverty History together, became one of many partners drawn from campaigning and aid organisations, faith groups, charities and unions. The triple aims of Aid, Debt and Trade bear comparison with the *shalom* or kingdom values of, respectively, mercy, forgiveness and justice. While acknowledging the potential risks involved, the 'with' element of initiating a response to an issue, but then becoming one partner or voice among many, is one I can identify with. Owing to the global scale of this project, 'presence-among' in a local sense is not a consideration.

Avec

Operating at a more local level and based on the work of sociologists T. R. and M. Batten who developed a 'non-directive approach' for group and community work,[6] George Lovell's 'Avec' model for community development contrasts working *for* and working *with* local community. Lovell argues that, while either may be more appropriate in a given circumstance, 'for' when used should be seen as a step towards 'with' as it reduces dependency, devolves power and responsibility, and promotes deeper relationships based on partnership rather than 'benefactor-beneficiary'. It also helps people 'acquire independence, status, a feeling of being wanted and of being useful and significant, as well as resolving the specific need'.[7]

Working *with* people generates a sense of community. It helps them to feel that they belong and that they are equal partners; they begin to talk in terms of 'we' instead of 'them and us'. It is *our* project instead of *their* project, *our* centre instead of *their* centre, *our* idea instead of *their* idea.[8]

While this is a clear 'with' methodology where 'the worker is in no sense in control',[9] having a lot in common with the praxis aspects of 'mission-with', it is more concentrated on general community development from a church base and does not specifically mention working with fellow residents on shared concerns arising out of being a 'presence-among'. It is actually the Battens who come closest to hinting at an incarnational model, writing of how 'a worker using the non-directive approach needs to be able to identify himself with his clients very fully'.[10] Still 'worker' and 'client', however. Though it is serving and 'helping others to ... realise how they can help themselves',[11] the help and learning is all one-way, from the church and its members to the people. It assumes churches 'already have a network of men and women, voluntary and full-time, within their organisational structure',[12] without any comment on the balance of such resources between inner-city and suburban areas.

Community ministry

This is a model of holistic mission developed by Ann Morisy,[13] who is concerned that Christian discipleship needs to deepen beyond 'being a law-abiding citizen who happens to go to church Sunday by Sunday and practices personal piety'.[14] She writes of community ministry ventures for those in a place of relative comfort and affluence as steps towards a possible more profound change in lifestyle and challenging of the assumptions of mainstream culture. Christians work alongside non-Christians on a 'Vocational Domain' which is 'the opportunity provided to enable people to respond to that sense within them that they could do more in their lives in relation to risk and concern for others'.[15]

This domain is also seen as being about 'encouraging and enabling people to express discipleship'[16] and to 'discover and embrace their vocation – their distinctive call from God'.[17] This is as much for non-Christians as for Christians as Morisy takes calling even further away than I have from an elitist within-Church notion to do with priesthood or ministry. Discipleship too (which she prefers to call 'Venturesome Love' to remove the connotation of 'doing jobs in church') is opened to all in a way not dissimilar to my recognition that acts of building *shalom* are not the exclusive preserve of Christians.

Morisy's model shares with 'mission-with' a wide definition of mission and several aspects of 'project-praxis', with emphasis on humility, vulnerability, relationships and partnership. However, what I would regard as a prerequisite for 'mission-with', namely 'presence-among', is missing. Ultimately, this is a journeying out from suburbia in which there is no notion of incarnational ministry, which may be seen as a step too far for Morisy's constituency, though far better this than nothing at all. While there is working with local contexts on an equal partnership, some distance is left between those contexts

231

and where Christians tend to live and go back to after working on a project with others. This leaves her model open to 'it's all right for you, you don't have to live here' criticism, a short step from 'us and them'.

The Isaiah Vision

Coming out of the World Council of Churches and advocated by Raymond Fung,[18] this is a strategy for local mission based on Isaiah's vision of a community characterised by long and healthy old age, no infant deaths, and where those who work receive the fruits of their labour.[19] As a *shalom*-building agenda that can be shared with other faiths and agencies, it can be worked on in partnership with others: 'Christians rejoice over the fact of our non-monopoly.'[20] There are many ways to work towards this dream, big and small, including an emphasis on 'Christian involvement as persons, families and small groups in the course of daily living'.[21] This inclusion of the ordinary is welcome, though the locations of those families and persons is not commented on – perhaps it is assumed. While being an end in itself, this working together is clearly also a means – as trust and friendship develops – to an evangelistic end of sharing the gospel in a more direct way. There also seems to be no mention of Christians joining in with expressions of this agenda initiated or already being run by others (though presumably this would not be inconsistent with this approach). While honesty, humility and vulnerability are encouraged as vital to the partner relationship, the initiative, invitation to partnership, and with it the control, remains with the Church.

Community Organising

A more political approach to working with others may be found in Community Organising. Schaller sees a Community Organiser as a 'change-agent', defined as an outsider coming in. Acting as a go-between between the community and the power structures, the organiser's role is to help identify issues, emphasise common objectives and focus discontent, and recruit and train indigenous leaders.[22] 'A successful community organiser will eventually work himself out of a job in that community.'[23] This also is a specific role, with a timescale and purpose, which can be useful and of great benefit to a community. I have used insights and principles from Community Organising in my own praxis (and salt and yeast are change-agents[24]). There is a 'with' aspect in that an organiser will begin with the issues identified as concerns by the community, but also a 'for' aspect in that he or she is working for and on behalf of the community. However, while an ordinary resident could be a change-agent and help organise their community, this involves some tweaking of the usual definition and relationship, which is more along the lines of a worker and client. It takes little account of the organiser being someone local who is there as a member of that community before and after a project's timespan. In addition, the organiser as an outsider coming in will have to make contacts, build relationships and earn trust from scratch, as well as persuade people with little confidence or motivation to take on a project. An insider, using some of the community organiser's methods, has a distinct advantage. As with the Avec model, there is much in common here with the second stage of 'mission-with', that of 'project-praxis', but the initial 'presence-among' stage, and the integrity and depth which that adds, is largely bypassed.

The New Parish

This model explores the missional dynamics of a local church rediscovering the importance of physical place and committing deeply to its neighbourhood in such a way that 'rooting together as a church community within a common proximity could tangibly demonstrate everyday acts of love.'[25] This re-invention of the concept of the parish counters the individualism and 'living above place' which have fragmented, distanced and *dis*-placed the Western Church. Such a local church is described as being *within* its local neighbourhood as a 'faithful presence'. In terms of 'mission-with', this can be seen as a corporate application of 'presence-among'. Everyday actions of the individual members – also faithfully present in the parish – are significant as life is lived alongside and concerns are shared with the other residents.

The potential of seven-day-a-week presence is clear.

> What if the only time the world gets to experience how we as church interact together is when we're putting on a good front on Sunday morning? Which requires people to come through the doors. What about Monday morning? What if the church was a demonstration of what it means to be human, in the world, in everyday life?[26]

While not urban specific, this model has been observed in a number of locations, including urban ones, with encouraging results. Should a church decide to implement this strategy, there will be implications for some members who would need to consider relocating into the neighbourhood.[27] Additionally, a new factor would be present in making decisions about moving away from the church's locality.

The classic missionary model

We now move to a second group of models that include relocation as a first step. There is a long tradition in the Christian Church of missionaries going out to other countries, peoples and cultures, and while there are a number of variations, the basic model involves living as an incomer in a community for a period of time. I have referred to Hudson Taylor's challenging of the accepted separatist approach of his contemporaries as he sought to identify more closely with the people he was working with, using the incarnation of Jesus as a model. This was the role model used by Martin Gooder as he drew parallels between the overseas mission field and the British inner city. Vincent Donovan took a further step away from traditional methods by deliberately allowing the Masai people to form Church around their culture, rather than making a Western model an inherent part of his gospel message. While these can be seen as 'mission-with' in terms of 'presence-among', and the parallel for any incoming praxis is useful, this is an incoming in a particular role with a specific intention of bringing a message 'to' and doing acts of service 'for'. The missioner is not present primarily as an ordinary resident.

Classic pastoral ministry

Alongside the classic missionary approach there is the classic pastoral approach to ministry, exemplified by the Anglican and Roman Catholic churches and their parish systems which clearly define a local area and community to be a 'presence-among' (this is not to exclude other churches, such as Methodist, which also operate on a geographical basis). Many church leaders, such as Martin Gooder, have made a commitment to living in the neighbourhoods and among the people they seek to serve, unlike other professionals visiting from nine to five, Monday to Friday. John Pridmore and Kenneth Leech are two from the Anglican Church who have written about their long-term service as parish priests living in inner-city parishes for many years.[28]

While being an outworking of the missional 'cure of souls', praxis is on a pastoral ministry basis, seeking to be and act 'with' the surrounding community through involvement in local organisations, advocacy, provision of services, as well as in personal ways with individuals.[29] However, while providing valuable service, often involving much personal sacrifice, owing to being present in a context in an official capacity, there is a difference in role, expectation (locally and from the employing institution) and perception to those of being an ordinary resident, which is how I have sought to live in my area. Pridmore, because of the pressures of inner-city ministry, advises regular time out of the parish to 'stay sane' and, when back, 'you must somehow maintain that distance inwardly'.[30] Additionally, owing to minimum requirements for clergy housing and other considerations such as security, it is usual, while being situated in the neighbourhood, for the rectory, vicarage, manse, etc to be physically different and separated from the other dwellings. Another difference is that in the cases of Pridmore and Leech, as with most clergy, they have moved in specifically to carry out a job and have moved out again, or retired to different areas, not necessarily in the inner city, when that job has come to an end (though it should be noted that there is an etiquette of leaving space for a successor when leaving a post).

A variation on the full-time clergy model is the introduction by the Anglican Church from the 1970s of several forms of 'auxiliary' or 'supplementary' ministry – Ordained Local, Non-Stipendary/Self-Supporting and Ordained Pioneer Ministers (OLM, NSM, SSM, OPM respectively) – where the minister is self-supporting through other employment. In some cases (not the OLM, which is an existing member of a congregation) this will involve being placed into a community, in much the same way as a full-time minister. While this can remove some of the distinctions between the minister and the other residents, for instance, through use of similar housing and perhaps a different form of presence through working locally, there are still those that result from the official role and expectations. And for many, but not all, this still includes relocating to carry out a job, and staying only for as long as that job lasts.

Church planting, Emerging Church

Though all churches were 'planted' at some time, 'church planting' became prominent in the 1990s through a concerted but ultimately disappointing effort to take Church closer to people geographically.[31] Seeking to learn from that previous experience is a movement that has been dubbed 'Emerging Church' – 'not quite the same as church planting, although planting is at the heart of it'.[32] It has been defined as 'missional communities arising from within post-modern culture and consisting of followers of Jesus who are seeking to be faithful in their place and time'.[33] Instead of cloning existing Church, it 'begins with the people church is seeking to reach',[34] taking Church into networks, to include being closer culturally. It is a multifaceted and disparate movement from which I shall concentrate on an instance that involves relocation into an inner-city context.

Urban Expression is a mission agency that 'recruits, equips, deploys and networks self-financing teams pioneering creative and relevant expressions of the Christian church in under-churched areas of the inner city'.[35] It seeks to challenge 'the trend of some Christians moving out of the cities and encourage Christians to relocate to the inner cities'.[36] High value is placed on building relationships from an incarnational base and a belief in 'doing things with and not just for communities, sharing our lives with others and learning from others who share their lives with us'.[37] Here is clear 'mission-with' praxis – 'presence-among' and working with. The difference to my experience is again in the intention behind the relocation, in this case to form a church (though it is more open-ended and flexible than the classic pastoral ministry model), and in there being a ready-made like-minded community within the community.

Missional community

As what some might regard as a variation on the above, some expressions of what has been called the 'New Monastic' movement involve deliberate relocation to inner-city areas. These include Shane Claiborne's 'Simple Way' in Philadelphia, and 'Urban Vision' in Wellington, New Zealand, who describe themselves as 'not superstars. We are just ordinary Wellingtonians from different walks of life, trying to live together in a way that embraces those in our neighborhoods who are struggling, living out the good news we have found'.[38]

As part of an earlier variation on this, Roman Catholic Passionist monk Austin Smith writes as a resident in an inner-city community, living in an ordinary house, rather than a presbytery or manse, with others as a missional community. However, he is also a priest and member of a religious order so, as with Pridmore and Leech, there are certain perceptions and expectations he has to work with. He writes of issues with getting beyond being defined by and restricted by his institutional role as a Christian minister and the assumptions that go with it. 'I am part of the furniture of a "Christian" society.'[39]

These expressions are closer to but still not the same as being simply a local resident, intentional or otherwise, and not part of a community within the community.

Christian relational youth work

I first came across this model when Urban Action Manchester (UAM) began in North Manchester in 1991. With workers encouraged to live in the same community, this is a holistic approach, enabling and encouraging young people to realise their own God-given worth and develop their potential.[40]

M13 Youth Project was set up in 1995 as a project of UAM by fellow long-term incomer, and member of Brunswick church, Helen Gatenby. It covers an area of Ardwick, which includes Chorlton-on-Medlock and describes itself as a 'community-based voluntary sector project ... specialising in street-based "detached" youth work with young people often labelled hard-to-reach'.[41] M13 works from a clear Christian ethos, including working for *shalom*, with young people, seeking to enable them to learn:

> We believe all young people deserve to be treated
> with respect and dignity and that each young person
> can love, think, create, reflect, enjoy, achieve and
> make a positive difference to their world.[42]

I was a trustee of M13 for a number of years and was influenced by these values, and Helen's determination for young people to be seen in a positive light, in what I sought to bring to the forming of Carisma. Helen lives in the same community as the young people she works with, and encourages other staff to do the same (to the point that most now are local young people the project has worked with). This is unlike most other professional youth workers, and controversially subverts accepted notions of 'professional distance', but over the years the value of this incarnational identification has been proven in the depth of the relationships built with young people, the reputation of the project locally, and the quality of its youth work, recognised by major funders.

'Mission-with' is evidenced here in the 'presence-among', both of workers and the organisation itself, and in a number of projects run with the young people which fit the 'project-praxis' part of the model. The differences with my experience are that again there is a specific role, and where workers have moved in to the area, it has been in order to perform that role and, with a couple of exceptions, there has been no long-term commitment beyond that time.

Eden projects

Eden is 'a network of church-linked youth and community projects located in some of Britain's most deprived neighbourhoods.'[43] Eden teams live as 'an intentional Christian presence with a particular emphasis on youth work in their communities'.[44] This is an incarnational model, asking for a minimum commitment of five years.

> What might be different about us is where and how we choose to live. Instead of looking for the best house we can find in the nicest area, we are putting roots down in areas that most people avoid. We do this because we have sensed a call from God to do something more for the young people and their families in the toughest areas.[45]

Particularly when it started, Eden's was a self-confessed 'hi-viz' approach,[46] which contrasts with the lower-profile 'mission-with'. From observation and speaking with members of early teams, there was an expectation that revival-type miracles would occur immediately and big changes in lives and communities would follow soon after, leading to some disillusionment when that did not happen. There were also issues with suspicion and hostility from the local people. Some hard lessons were learned with characteristic energy as the project has matured, and I now discern a softer, more humble and inclusive attitude. Miracles have not been ruled out, but there is a more realistic approach to timescale and the difficulties of the context, and a respect for and willingness to work with those who already live there. A 'with' mindset is now encouraged, over against a 'to' or 'for'. Former Eden director Matt Wilson puts it like this:

> It's really not acceptable for us to act as if the people in the communities we locate into are somehow generic human units that we can just 'do our ministry TO'. And actually neither is it really satisfactory for us to offer a whole bunch of stuff FOR people in the community – however easy it is to baptize such activity in the language of 'serving'. Our aspiration should always be to draw alongside people in the community as neighbours and friends rather than 'service providers' (in a 'paraklete' sort of way?) in order to work out together WITH them how we can all together live well and thrive in the light of God's hope and love.[47]

Elsewhere Matt writes that a result of this sort of equal 'with' relationship will be happening in both directions.

> If we adopt this mindset then we recognise that following Jesus is a journey that involves growing in companionship with all sorts of people, many of whom are not like us one bit. ... As we pursue the mission of God in our neighbourhood, we open ourselves up to the possibility that we might learn from those we thought we'd be teaching, and may be blessed by those we thought we'd be blessing.[48]

Researching the experience of Eden team members, Anna Ruddick notes a 'movement in self-understanding from missionary to neighbour'[49] as daily life in the urban community has challenged expectations and assumptions and learning and unlearning has taken place. With Eden's background also being evangelical, this is an interesting transition, moving the team members' self-awareness closer to what mine has been since the early years – that of being first a resident who is a Christian. Like them, I have had much to learn and can identify with fellow Christian incomers who, 'through cross-cultural relocation, have had not only their culture but their theology called into question'.[50]

Despite this emphasis on making a deprived area 'home', and encouraging team members to see themselves as residents, a strong overtly missional element remains important. So, once moved in, team members will quickly be proactive in getting to know local young people and setting up pieces of work with them.

While this model shares a lot in common with my experience, there are several differences. We are primarily residents in a single household, like those around us, and not part of a community within the community, and we are not youth workers. A further difference is in how we have lived in our bit of urban context, which could be summed up as lower profile and missionally more responsive than proactive.

Long-term Christian incomers

While in some instances of relocation there may be an initial intention to remain for a long period, this is not so much a model as a state which evolves as time goes by. It is hard to say at which point the phrase 'long-term' applies,[51] but it could apply to any of the models above that involves relocating to a deprived area, whether with a particular role, project or timescale in mind, which over time turns into a longer commitment, eclipsing the original purpose of the move. It could also include a simple moving in to live there, not linked to a job or project – which was my original intention – and staying.

Bob Holman was an example of a long-term Christian incomer who moved to inner-city Glasgow in 1987, giving up his post as a professor at Bath University to do so. He worked mostly in Easterhouse, setting up FARE (Family Action in Rogerfield and Easterhouse) and advocating and campaigning politically on behalf of the local communities. Holman's achievements – for which he was awarded, and turned down, an MBE – were many, and he was an inspiring example of response to a call to incarnational living in a deprived area. Perhaps closest to my experience in terms of time spent and not being there in an official capacity, Holman did, however, work in a more high-profile way than I do and took much more of a leadership and entrepreneurial role in his community. This approach, also taken by a friend and fellow long-term incomer in Manchester who for a number of years ran the charity Healthy Ardwick, is different to mine. While including strong elements of 'with' and empowerment, this is more of an initiative-taking 'mission-for' methodology, driving a specific agenda.

Conclusion

While there are elements in all of the models above that, to varying degrees, I can identify with and draw from, none is an exact fit to my experience as a mission-practitioner. The closest are those which involve the missioner physically relocating to the urban context and also using a 'with' way of working. This should not be taken as a criticism or putting down of any of these models as inferior, as all have been and will continue to be used by God as part of a rich variety of approaches to mission matched to an equally varied number of contexts, circumstances and people.

All the models involve a specific role or task or taking action or a way of doing and, in many where relocation is a part, are linked to or necessitated by that role or task. I, on the other hand, did not move into this community to 'do' anything, with any task in mind, or in a timeframe dictated by a project. I certainly did not come here because of an official role of any sort. A further important difference with some of the models is with a role being that of a salaried professional with implied pressure to show results. Though working with a Christian urban charity, I am not paid to live here or to get involved in local projects, which gives me a degree of independence others may not have.[52]

Common to several of these models where relocation is involved is the notion of bivocational working. The additional vocation, supported by the existing job or career beyond the context relocated to, is seen in terms of a role or task in the context, carried out by the bivocational worker as a resident. This could be pastoral ministry as a Non-Stipendary Minister or youth work as an Eden team member. Eden uses the term 'urban tentmaking' after Paul in Acts 18:3. 'The vast majority of our Eden team members work at some profession or career in order to pay the bills and give surplus time to work with the team, reaching nearby young people and their families.'[53] I would see the vocation primarily as simply living there, emphasising *being* rather than doing.

There is a contrast between a proactive methodology of many of these models and my more reactive – maybe even verging on reticent – approach, what I have called 'intentional passivity', coming out of self-identification as a resident who is a Christian. If the missioner is moving into an area with a job to do or a specific project in mind, then he or she will want, or be expected if there is a sending agency, to get on with it. This is more of the usual 'mission-for' way of working but, in an inner-city setting, there needs to be awareness of the dangers of creating dependence and reinforcing disempowerment. Perhaps the question should be asked, and the possibility added to the list of approaches, whether a process of waiting and watching and getting to know, while taking more time, would lead to projects emerging from the life of the community that are owned by and empower local people.

Thus 'mission-with' could enhance some of the models. Where the missioner's daily life is observable, and he or she is aware of the potential value of the ordinary, this can add to the credibility of their role, task or project – 'mission-with' personal praxis earning the right for 'mission-for' or 'mission-to'. Part of that awareness needs to be that the effect can also be a negative. In an 'incoming' situation, especially to an inner-city community where a history of estrangement from the Church can mean an initial suspicion – if not hostility – care, caution, humility and patience are vital. This can be exacerbated in a team or community approach to Christian incoming, common to several of the models, where an incoming group, at a certain size, can initially be perceived as a threat by local people. This approach can also be open to criticism as 'colonisation'. Our moving in, by contrast, was as an individual household, and members of a local church.

Writing about his pioneering work in Soho, Ken Leech notes the default hostility of the local young people towards the 'crusaders who come to the clubs in order to convert, rescue and save them'. As advocated above, Ken used a waiting and watching strategy:

> For nearly a year I used to sit drinking coffee, deliberately not speaking to people unless they spoke first, and simply trying to become part of the

scenery. Once one is accepted as a trustworthy and reliable person, there are endless possibilities and ways of helping which may arise. But one needs first to establish one's role. For the Christian, this is to carry the love of Christ in one's humanity and by one's presence to enable others to feel his care for them. This is as often achieved in silence as in much speaking.[54]

Sam Wells identifies three ways of engaging with others: working *for*, working *with*, and *being with*. He then points out that in the life of Jesus He spent a week working for us in Jerusalem – doing what we could not, achieving our salvation, preceded by three ministry years working with us – calling people to follow and work alongside Him. But before that 'he spent 30 years in Nazareth *being with* us, setting aside his plans and strategies, and experiencing in his own body not just the exile and oppression of the children of Israel, but also the joy and sorrow of family and community life'.[55]

That is 90 per cent being with, 10 per cent working with or for. With our fixation on doing and activity and roles, do we tend to get this emphasis the other way round?

---

[1] Bosch, *Transforming Mission*, p.512.

[2] Daniel Strange, 'Co-belligerence and Common Grace: Can the Enemy of My Enemy Be My Friend?' *Cambridge Papers*, Vol. 14, no. 3, 2005, p.1.

[3] Francis Schaeffer, *Plan for Action: An Action Alternative Handbook for Whatever Happened to the Human Race?* (Old Tappan, NJ: Revell, 1980) p.68.

[4] These are British examples. Co-belligerence has been influential in the USA as a model used by the Christian Right to pursue a moralist agenda.

[5] Langlois lists several dangers and strategies to counter them, which include not trusting the co-belligerents. John Langlois, 'Co-Belligerency: Right or Wrong?' quoted in *Cambridge Papers*, 2005, p.4.

[6] T. R. and M. Batten, *The Non-Directive Approach* (London: Avec Publications, 1988). An abridged version of T. R. and M. Batten, *The Non-Directive Approach in Group and Community Work* (Oxford: University Press, 1967). This model has a lot in common with Community Organising below.

[7] Lovell, *Church and Community Development*, p.14.

[8] Lovell, *Church and Community Development*, p.5.

[9] Batten, *The Non-Directive Approach*, p.12. This echoes Chalke's definition of true incarnation.

[10] Batten, *The Non-Directive Approach*, p.20.

[11] Lovell, *Church and Community Development*, p.49.

[12] Lovell, *Church and Community Development*, p.3.

[13] Frost and Hirsch's 'shared projects' share several features with Morisy's model. 'Shared projects allow the Christians to partner with unbelievers in useful, intrinsically valuable activities within the community. ... The church can initiate ... or simply get behind existing projects.' Frost and Hirsh, *Shaping of Things to Come*, p.25.

[14] Morisy, *Beyond the Good Samaritan*, p.13.

[15] Morisy, *Journeying Out*, p.241. This, together with a 'Foundational Domain' (to do with helping people explore the possibility of God), are two areas the Church needs to put more resources into as they can serve the 'Explicit Domain' of core teaching and practice.

[16] Morisy, *Journeying Out*, p.218.

[17] Morisy, *Journeying Out*, p,204. This echoes Luther's notion of vocation.

[18] Raymond Fung, *The Isaiah Vision: An Ecumenical Strategy for Congregational Evangelism* (Geneva: WCC Publications, 1992).

[19] Isaiah 65:20-21.

[20] Fung, The Isaiah Vision, p.7.

[21] Fung, The Isaiah Vision, p.50.

[22] Linthicum sees Nehemiah as a Community Organiser. Linthicum, *Building a People of Power*, p.118ff.

[23] Lyle E. Schaller, *Community Organisation: Conflict and Reconciliation* (Nashville: Abingdon Press, 1966) p.45.

[24] Matthew 5:13; 13:33.

[25] Paul Sparks, Tim Soerens, Dwight J. Friesen, *The New Parish: How Neighbourhood Churches are Transforming Mission, Discipleship and Community* (Downer's Grove, Il.: InterVarsity Press, 2014), p.139.

[26] Paul Sparks, Faithful Presence conference, Birmingham, 9th November 2016.

[27] 'What would the Church look like if we chose to buy homes in the same streets and subdivisions, the same buildings and blocks, the same suburbs and sections? What would our love look like if it showed up dozens of times a week in small but profound ways: meals cooked, prayers prayed, songs sung, Scripture studied, games played, parties thrown, tears shed, reconciliation practiced, resources given?' Sparks, Soerens, Friesen, *The New Parish*, p.139, quoting Jon Tyson. Intriguing questions, though the list of actions maybe implies initiative-taking 'for' rather than joining-in 'with'.

[28] John Pridmore, *The Inner-City of God: The Diary of an East End Parson* (London: Canterbury Press, 2008); Kenneth Leech, *Doing Theology in Altab Ali Park* (London: Darton, Longman & Todd, 2006).

[29] Leech specifically draws a distinction between ministry 'to' and 'with'. Leech, *Doing Theology in Altab Ali Park*, p.50.

[30] Pridmore, *Inner-City of God*, p.137.

[31] Moynagh notes 'great hopes for church planting' in the early 1990s. 'Some thought that 20,000 new churches could be launched in the UK by the end of the century. In the event, between 1989 and 1998 only 1,867 churches opened in England, while 2,757 closed.' Michael Moynagh, *emergingchurch.intro* (Oxford: Monarch, 2004) p.21.

[32] Moynagh, *emergingchurch.intro*, p.21. There are a number of other labels such as the Anglican 'Fresh Expressions of Church' which coexist as a 'mixed economy of church' alongside existing parishes.

[33] Eddie Gibbs and Ryan K. Bolger, *Emerging Churches: Creating Christian Community in Postmodern Cultures* (London: SPCK, 2006) p.28.

[34] Moynagh, *emergingchurch.intro*, p.22.

[35] http://www.urbanexpression.org.uk (accessed 6th October 2016).

[36] http://urbanexpression.org.uk/our-values/relationship/ (accessed 6th October 2016).

[37] http://urbanexpression.org.uk/our-values/relationship/ (accessed 6th October 2016).

[38] Jenny and Justin Duckworth, *Against the Tide, Towards the Kingdom*, p.xvi.

[39] Austin Smith, *Passion for the Inner City* (London: Sheed & Ward, 1983) p.79.

[40] Other examples of this holistic way of working are Frontier Youth Trust, http://www.fyt.org.uk and Oxford Youth Works http://www.oxfordyouthworks.co.uk (accessed 11th October 2016).

[41] http://www.m13youthproject.org.uk (accessed 6th October 2016).

[42] http://www.m13youthproject.org.uk (accessed 6th October 2016).

[43] The first Eden project began in Wythenshawe, Manchester, in 1997. They are now in 22 locations around Greater Manchester

and in six other cities around the country including London, Liverpool, Hull and Sheffield, forming what is now known as the Eden Network, www.eden-network.org/ (accessed 6th October 2016).

[44] Anna E. Ruddick (née Thompson), 'Holy Sofas: Transformational Encounters between Evangelical Christians and Post-Christendom Urban Communities', *Practical Theology* 5, no. 1, 2012, p.47.

[45] http://dioceseofyork.org.uk/news-events/news/concrete-faith/ (accessed 6th October 2016).

[46] Wilson, *Eden: Called to the Streets*, p.88.

[47] Email from Matt Wilson, 17th June 2010.

[48] Matt Wilson, *Concrete Faith: The Inside Story of the Eden Network* (Manchester: Message Trust, 2012) p.144.

[49] Ruddick, 'Holy Sofas', p.50.

[50] Ruddick, 'Holy Sofas', p.60.

[51] Overseas mission agencies define 'long-term' from a matter of months up to five years.

[52] An exception was Carisma, for which it was agreed with the Urban Presence trustees to include a part of my time commitment in my work portfolio.

[53] http://eden-network.org/join-the-movement/urban-tentmaking (accessed 6th October 2016).

[54] Kenneth Leech, *4 Youth on the Drift*, 2010, http://www.drugtext.org/pdf/Keep-The-Faith-Baby/4-youth-on-the-drift.pdf (accessed 1st December 2015). Part of this quote was used in Fr Leech's obituary in *The Times*, 29th September 2015, http://www.thetimes.co.uk/tto/opinion/obituaries/article4 571384.ece (accessed 6th October 2016).

[55] Sam Wells, *The Nazareth Manifesto* (Durham, NC: Duke University, 2008), https://web.duke.edu/kenanethics/Nazareth Manifesto_SamWells.pdf (accessed 6th October 2016).

Conclusions
'Mission-with': something out of the ordinary

Introduction

I have been attempting to explain 'mission-with' as a specific model of mission, separate from, but hopefully complementary to, the more common 'mission-for' and 'mission-to'. 'Mission-with' requires close connection with a community, a 'presence-among', out of which arises 'project-praxis' with and alongside others. 'Mission-with' can be effective in communicating gospel-infused values and lifestyle, through attitude, demeanour and responses, as the missioner engages in everyday activities and shared projects among, alongside, in relation to and observed by, other local residents. Given a 'wide' definition of mission this is therefore missional.

'Presence-among' and 'project-praxis' are the two 'mission-with' stages, rather than elements, as one develops out of the other. Shared projects, where there is equal partnership and *shalom*-building, can happen in other ways, but for my definition of 'project-praxis', the ingredient of shared concern through personal experience of the issue must be present, and for this, 'presence-among' is necessary.

My personal experience has shown that it is possible to live and raise a family in the inner city while also engaging deeply in a relational and missional sense with such a community and to become an agent of the kingdom of God and the building of *shalom*. This path necessarily involves being present in a neighbourhood long term, and becoming bicultural to the point of 'going native' to some extent.

A significant part of my story and experience has been relocation and becoming a Christian incomer in a deprived inner-city community with a cross-cultural dynamic, where particular social factors have been present, such as pluralism, poverty, injustice, gang violence, lack of confidence, low self-esteem, disempowerment and greater estrangement from Church and Christian faith than in, say, Manchester's suburbia. This has provided the background to the praxis reflected on in this research, resulting in the 'mission-with' model. My experience of the inner city has been important in challenging my middle-class evangelicalism, with its methodology, cultural assumptions and clear-cut definitions, and opening me up to seek a model of mission to explain the 'with' praxis I found myself doing (the 'theological back-fill' referred to at the start of the book).

Even though relocation is not essential to the model, 'mission-with' emphasises the 'where' (or 'with whom') of calling, reflecting the incarnational sending and identifying aspects of mission. It is possible, therefore, that adoption of 'mission-with' will lead to a review of 'where' and a questioning of the cultural assumptions that lie behind the tendency for Christians to move to or stay in the suburbs. Anyone conducting such a review prayerfully may discover a fresh calling to those places where the Christian 'presence-among' is weak and certain skills and resources are comparatively underdeveloped and in short supply.

What has been underlined to me through writing this book, and at a number of key points in the past, has been that the essence of our call is to simply 'be' here. Not in some disconnected 'zen' sense, but living a life, doing the ordinary things that people do – that we would be doing wherever we lived – fully engaged with the other people around who are also doing these things. Being part of a community, being a resident, being a Christian who is 'present-among'. The mission is first of all in that personal praxis, not in a role, task or project. Such projects that have come about have been born directly out of that shared life and a shared desire to take action on shared concerns.

What this means is that 'mission-with' does not require a qualification, official role, job interview, training or skill – as, say, a youth worker – or an entrepreneurial flair. In a sense, this is 'mission for the rest of us', but more than that, containing basic elements of mission available for all who are trying to follow Jesus. The only qualification needed is to be there, as a resident and a neighbour.

Evaluation

'Presence-among'

- Our decision to live here was based on a sense of call as a missional phenomenon. A strength of 'mission-with' is a restoration of location (or 'where') as a vital part of calling and discipleship: being in the right place to serve. Being here has been the prerequisite and starting point for any resulting missional praxis. We are, first, residents of an inner-city community, and second, missioners in any proactive or overt sense of the term, but always both. A strength of 'presence-among' is in recognising that everyday actions and encounters, where we interact, serve, or are served, carry potential missional significance as an outworking of God's call, transforms them into something else, touching on the mystery of God at work in us and in our neighbours, fulfilling the *missio Dei*. However, a corresponding weakness is that as a resident without a particular role or task I run the risk of getting so settled into routine life in the community – taking 'going native' too far – that my personal praxis ends up losing any distinctive missional edge. This is a danger generally of long-term, low-profile praxis without a specific mission event or activity running with a timetable, goals and expectations to focus on and look to for motivation. This is where it is vital to also be an active part of a supportive local church that recognises the missional role of its locally based members where they are living their normal lives. Supportive to the point, perhaps, of prioritising equipping, encouraging and refreshing its members in this role over recruiting them as workers for church activities.

- A strength of 'presence-among', especially in multicultural areas or among people more distanced from the Church, is its low-profile approach – 'intentional passivity' – learning, identifying, building relationship, earning the right to share faith overtly. Some Christians, however, may criticise this approach as not direct enough or too slow or diluted. 'Mission-with' could in theory be misused as a means or shortcut to another end, such as a more direct or overt form of mission or evangelism – the bait on the hook. Regardless of how sincere the motives, this can be a recipe for problems and negative outcomes leading to loss of trust and integrity, particularly in a multi-ethnic area like inner-south Manchester where great sensitivity is required. However, given that the missioner will be a member of the local community, and therefore the first recipient of any reaction, it is to be hoped that they will have the integrity and wisdom to use 'mission-with' as an end in itself, and the patience to wait. If it is creating the 'fascination' that Kreider talks about, mission of a more overt kind will follow naturally rather than being forced.

- Another strength of 'presence-among', as I have experienced it, is in being an individual household among other households and not part of a larger group. This Christian incoming is not going into a place in any sense that could be perceived as 'mob-handed', as a community within the community, or with any risk of colonisation. The weakness of this approach is in the risks of isolation and lack of accountability, which is where the support of being part of a team or sub-community can help. In our case, being part of a local church and being in contact with other fellow incomers has been important.

'Project-praxis'

- Working with others on issues they see as important, as equal partners, develops relationships, trust and confidence. Achieving some success not only improves the lot of local residents, but also builds confidence and self-esteem further – in some individuals, dramatically. In a community where such things are lacking, this is a positive result, and manifests *shalom*. A weakness in 'project-praxis' lies in the risk of getting over-involved in the issue and becoming less aware of the *shalom* aspect or the distinctive contribution Christians can bring.

- As shown in the projects described above, it is possible for something that is not explicitly Christian to nevertheless be influenced in the development of its ethos, values and way of working through the involvement of individual Christians. It also demonstrates that Christians can be involved in a project for its own sake and as simply part of the group without having to be in charge or controlling the project. This strength is mirrored by the potential risks of not being in control. I have referred above to situations where the project going in directions that a Christian cannot support was a potential problem. Is such vulnerability, however, a negative thing or a necessary dynamic of equal partnership?

- Working with others of various faiths and none on projects aiming to improve the well-being of local people, everyone's action is *shalom*-building. In the light of the *missio Dei*, such praxis is missional, and not the preserve of the Church. However, there are still aspects that are dependent on Christian faith, such as awareness of serving God's purposes, and an understanding of the nature of problems as symptomatic of the deeper issue of estrangement from God, and the gospel as a resource towards finding solutions. Even with this proviso, 'project-praxis' is open to being misunderstood by fellow Christians, particularly by those with a narrower definition and theology of mission. This could be expressed in a prioritising of other forms of mission, or a criticism that, if everything is regarded as mission, then nothing is. Being in the outer, *missio Dei* circle, of Ferdinando's four concentric circles of mission, and therefore furthest out from the clearly defined centre and operating at the edges of what could be seen as missional, involves some risks. Where spiritual impact is the primary measure of effectiveness, those advocating a form of mission that is much harder to quantify, could find themselves, with their model, on the margins of church priorities and mission praxis respectively.

> Sure we have precious stories of transformation in the lives of our neighbors and in our own lives. But these don't usually match up to the big expectations of 'successful mission' and don't offer us positions of power or influence, even in the church.[1]

This has also been my experience.

Application

Who and where

If calling and mission is for all Christians, that does not equate to advocating 'mission-with' as a model for everyone at all times. As I have experienced it and reflected on it, in an inner-city community, 'presence-among' ideally requires a long-term commitment. However, as no two communities are the same, that may not necessarily be the case elsewhere. Additionally, a number of factors may limit the ability to be 'simply' a resident, such as having an official role (eg a priest or a councillor), or a job that requires a lot of travelling – which was my situation for much of the first 12 years here. In another context different forms of mission may be more appropriate, though attitudes of respect and humility, the importance of relationship, and praxis as *shalom*-building could apply anywhere. Similarly, a generous definition of mission that allows for the actions of others to be counted as *shalom*-building, even if they do not acknowledge it as such, is something that has a wide application.

I have concentrated in this book on geographical community and in a particular inner-city area. In other types of community, such as sparse rural, suburban or dormitory towns, the nature of 'presence-among' will be very different, and here other variations such as leisure-club chaplaincy and network churches come into play. Exploring 'mission-with' principles in another type of area or different contexts such as work communities or interest networks, where it could be argued a missioner is 'incarnate' through role rather than place, is another study.

Relating to 'mission-for' and 'mission-to'

'Mission-with' is not meant to replace other forms of mission, which I have summarised as 'mission-to' and 'mission-for' and are characterised as more direct and missioner or church-initiated and led. 'Mission-with' can be an effective complementary mission approach for local churches to put alongside those approaches. As they tend to be more intermittent and project-led, 'mission-with', as an ongoing, low-level praxis in the background, can be a bridge to doing 'mission-to' or 'mission-for' with integrity built on a foundation of real partnership and equality of relationship with the community, built over time and stemming from the presence of church members living locally. It is not an either/or but a both/and. While both are, of course, of value, 'mission-to' is church-initiated, hosted and controlled, and can by definition be done only by Christians; 'mission-for', where partnership does exist, is usually with the church exercising power. In situations where those methods would be inappropriate, 'mission-with' can act as a preparation, earning the right to share the good news of the gospel with integrity built on trusting relationship (and hopefully with a degree of 'fascination' present). This is not a third stage to 'mission-with', but a transition into another form of mission, be it 'mission-for' or 'mission-to'.

This can legitimately be seen as an expression of Christian mission, as it moves people and communities closer to God's desired *shalom*. Though that activity is, and must be, an end in itself, it can also become a means towards, or earning the right, to share gospel realities more overtly (as in the 'Isaiah Vision'). Activities initiated and run by the local church – or one of its members as an individual activist – will be more likely to be trusted and participated in if they are in a context of ongoing 'mission-with', where that church or individual is seen as being 'one of us'.

The role of the local church

A limitation of 'mission-with' is that it applies more readily to individuals than in a corporate sense, though there is a case for seeing a church with a long history of service in a community, based on a high proportion of members living locally, having a corporate 'presence-among'.[2] Several of the church leaders interviewed in my 2010 survey spoke of the high regard their churches were held in by the local community, pointing to evidence such as lack of vandalism.[3]

In terms of 'project-praxis' there will be issues for a church acting as guest rather than host and in partnering on an equal basis when a project is based on its premises. However, a church can recognise 'mission-with' dynamics through releasing its members to, say, volunteer at another organisation's youth club (instead of starting its own – which may be problematical for those who regard a 'God-spot' as a non-negotiable) or serve on a tenants' and residents' association, seeing those roles as just as important as running a church-based activity or being on the church council.

Even more crucially, a church can come to recognise the importance of the day-to-day witness of its members as 'presence-among' in the local area. An individual Christian living in a particular place is very likely practising 'mission-with' to some extent – almost definitely through personal praxis and maybe also in 'project-praxis' – but perhaps without realising it. The first step is to be aware of the nature of actions, such as getting ten households to sign a letter to get a street light fixed, or lending a neighbour a spanner (or borrowing one), as being missional just as much, if in a different way, as inviting that neighbour to the Carol Service. The church can support this praxis. For instance, could the Sunday service feature the sharing of stories and prayers coming out of people's lives, jobs, concerns for neighbours, school friends and workmates as a major part of the worship, and not just a few lines in the Intercessions?[4] It is significant that none of the 'mission-with' praxis described in this book has been initiated by, or part of the programme of, a church. This points to a whole realm of missional engagement in the community by church members, which can be supported as such and built on by that church.

Significance and implications

'Mission-with' is a way of conceiving and thinking about mission which has a number of serious implications. Whereas much mission praxis is episodic – a project, event or campaign – 'mission-with' is an 'always on' model. As such it fits into a discipleship model where following Jesus impinges on every aspect of life and not just Sundays. It constitutes the missional aspect of daily living in a particular place alongside others who can observe our attitudes and responses.

It includes the praxis of others in aspects of the *missio Dei*. This is a significant departure from traditional thinking, especially in evangelical circles, where mission is limited to 'making disciples' and exclusively the task of the Church. Although the commission of the Church to make disciples still stands, mission is a much richer phenomenon, stemming from God's missionary desire to reach out to, and relate with, His creation and bring *shalom*.

Accepting this requires a new way of thinking for the Church, not just about mission, but by implication about our role in the world and our attitude to others. This should be characterised by honesty and humility as part of a more realistic view of ourselves as 'beggars showing other beggars where to find bread'. We should not be afraid to be transparent and vulnerable as redeemed, yet still fallible, humans, which will move us away from a compulsion to attempt to hide from society's gaze failure and sin when it inevitably happens.

Such a positive development moves us pastorally to a more honest praxis where the constraint to learn, mature and 'not grow weary in doing good'[5] is balanced against God's grace and unlimited forgiveness. This would free us to recover from tragedy and disappointment in our own time and see struggle and doubt as part of the journey of faith rather than weakness. Missionally, the 'holier-than-thou' and 'do-gooder' stereotypes would be challenged, and people would find it much easier to identify with and relate to Christians as like them but hopefully hinting at something more: the treasure in these fragile earthen vessels.[6] The potential significance for a much-needed shift in how the Church is perceived cannot be overstated.

We will become truly incarnational, and echo the mission of Christ, only when we have the courage to

> lift our eyes from the needs of our churches and
> congregations to serve our whole communities –
> giving up control and working as part of them rather
> than apart from them. This will be costly. It will hurt,
> and it will make us vulnerable – and therefore more
> effective.[7]

When a neighbour asked me how the loss of our son had affected my faith, the question arose out of genuine concern and curiosity. My answer did not minimise the doubts and struggles, but I was able to speak of the positives. For me, this is an illustration of 'mission-with'. On the basis of a relationship between our families over many years, we were able to share with honesty and depth (a year later it was our turn to comfort her when her mother died). In contrast, someone cold-calling at her door with a leaflet from the church that meets in the community centre a couple of streets away, none of whom live in the area, is 'mission-to'. While it was undoubtedly a sincere outreach, the lack of relationship behind it begs the question: who reaches her more deeply?

At a personal level, 'mission-with' praxis causes a re-evaluation of our lifestyle as Christians who are 'present-among'. This will mean abandoning the praxis of mission solely as bursts of activity carried out from a safe and impersonal distance. Instead, we will be open to scrutiny in seeking to bring missional intentionality to everyday life. While this does not mean that the Christian's everyday life did not have missional implications before, 'mission-with' means recognising that one's actions – all of them, all of the time – have missional significance. Will this result in 'onlookers inspecting our lifestyle and wagging their heads as they find it no different than their own',[8] or will it be a generator of 'fascination'? It may well lead to an honest reappraisal as we begin to explore the implications, as well as identify and confront values that have led us to, in Sine's words, 'work the Jesus stuff in round the sides' of our chosen lifestyles.[9]

If, as Martin Gooder says, the priority should be our calling and service of God, then other considerations, such as career, should be secondary. In a conversation with someone who was applying for teaching jobs, I asked if he felt called to stay in the area and at his church. He replied, 'Yes, but being realistic, in today's climate, if I get a job offer in another city, I would have to take it.' God may well lead people in this way, but the implication was that a job offer took precedence, while considering a call of God as a factor in where he lived was not 'realistic'. Of course, considering a call of God to teaching has to be weighed against this, but did thinking about it in any way other than economic even occur to him? Following Jesus is about taking a radically different approach to the 'all these things' referred to in Matthew 6:33. Unrealistic? Idealistic? Foolish? Especially 'in today's climate'? It would not be the first time the message of the cross – the biggest reversal of all – had been called 'foolish'.[10] I know of Christian incomers with professional qualifications who have taken shop jobs and turned down promotions or job offers that entailed moving in order to stay *where* they felt called by God to be – where, they could say with confidence, God had placed them.

The issue is whether following Jesus actually works in real life. It is either impractical, ridiculous, unrealistic idiocy – and, by implication this teacher and His followers are idealists who are out of touch with the real world – or it contains something of the mystery and wisdom of God: gaining by losing, the message of the cross. There is only one way to find out if it is true, and that involves faith, risk, possibly looking foolish, and reaching beyond our own resources. Vincent calls losing one's life in order to gain it 'the willingness to take the chance that the method of Jesus would actually work'.[11]

This was what we began to do all those years ago, trying to respond to an imbalance of where Christians lived in Manchester, and to be neighbours of and missioners *with* local people. We have made mistakes and have tried to learn from them, made more mistakes and learned again, tried to serve and be served, and had our share of joys and sorrows, successes and disappointments. But we do not regret coming here.

I have moved from a suspicion to the conviction that there is a different way to live, serve and witness as a Christian disciple. For more than 35 years we have been living out an experiment in establishing what that looks like. It has led to this model of mission praxis called 'mission-with', arising out of our long-term 'presence-among' a community in a deprived area. Though this is still, like us, a work in progress, it has proved effective in building *shalom* with others in this context.

Is 'mission-with' a model for the Church to recognise as an equally valid expression of mission to place alongside others and use to widen and deepen its mission praxis? I think it is.

[1] Jenny and Justin Duckworth, *Against the Tide, Towards the Kingdom*, p.43. See also Sara Jane Walker's comment, noted earlier: 'Church life rewards us for being self-starters, group leaders and those that make things happen.'

[2] See 'The New Parish' above.

[3] A survey of local people asking them to rate facilities in the neighbourhood gave Brunswick Church a 95 per cent favourable rating: testimony to the many years of faithful ministry and service. *Brunswick Neighbourhood Regeneration Project*, prepared for Manchester City Council by BMG research, June 2008.

[4] I remember asking in my own church some years ago why we prayed regularly in services for a missionary who taught in a school in Chile, but never for a congregation member who taught in a difficult inner-city school a couple of miles away!

[5] 2 Thessalonians 3:13 (ESV UK).

[6] After 2 Corinthians 4:7. This, of course, will be greatly facilitated by our living next door and sharing life's experiences.

[7] Chalke, *Intelligent Church*, p.114.

[8] Morisy, *Journeying Out*, p.96.

[9] Tom Sine, 'Cultural Values'.

[10] 1 Corinthians 1:23-27. Paul goes on in several Jesus-like reversals to contrast the foolishness and wisdom of God with that of the world, and how 'God chose the foolish things of the world to shame the wise', 1:27 (NCV).

[11] Vincent, 'Losing Life, Gaining Life' p.75.

So here's what I want you to do,
God helping you:
Take your
everyday,
ordinary
life –
your sleeping,
eating,
going-to-work,
and walking-around
life –
and place it before God as an offering.

Embracing what God does for you
is the best thing you can do for him.
Don't become so well-adjusted to your culture
that you fit into it without even thinking.
Instead, fix your attention on God.
You'll be changed from the inside out.
Readily recognize what he wants from you,
and quickly respond to it.
Unlike the culture around you,
always dragging you down
to its level of immaturity,
God brings the best out of you,
develops well-formed maturity in you.

Romans 12:1-2, *The Message*

Bibliography

Adamson, Tony. *Inner-City Evangelism: A Personal Reflection*. Nottingham: Grove Books, 1993.

Allis, Sam. 'How to Start a Ceasefire: Learning from Boston.' *Time Magazine*, 21st July 1997. http://www.time.com/time/magazine/article/0,9171,986710-1,00.html

Archbishop of Canterbury's Commission on Urban Priority Areas. *Faith in the City*. London: Church House Publishing, 1985.

Batten, T. R., and M. *The Non-Directive Approach*. London: Avec Publications, 1988.

Best, Ernest. *Following Jesus: Discipleship in the Gospel of Mark*. Sheffield: University of Sheffield, 1981.

Bosch, David J. *Transforming Mission: Paradigm Shifts in Theology of Mission*. Maryknoll, NY: Orbis, 1991.

Brandt, Cindy. *How I Kissed Evangelizing Goodbye*. 11th August 2014 http://cindywords.com/how-i-kissed-evangelism-goodbye

Broomhall, Marshall. *The Jubilee Story of the China Inland Mission*. London: Marshall, Morgan & Scott, 1915.

Brown, Colin, ed. *The New International Dictionary of New Testament Theology*. Carlisle: Paternoster, 1986.

Brueggemann, Walter. *The Word That Redescribes the World: The Bible and Discipleship*. Minneapolis: Fortress, 2006.

Calhoun, Craig, ed. *Dictionary of the Social Sciences*. Oxford: University Press, 2002.

Chalke, Steve. *Intelligent Church: A Journey Towards Christ-centred Community*. Grand Rapids, MI: Zondervan, 2006.

Cleverly, Charlie. *Epiphanies of the Ordinary: Encounters that change lives*. London: Hodder & Stoughton, 2012.

Coughlan C. P. *A Study to detect the magnitude of the youth crime problem in the North West of England*. A dissertation submitted to the University of Manchester for the degree of MRes in the Faculty of Social Sciences and Law, 2003.

Cranfield, C. E. B. *The Gospel According to St Mark*. Cambridge: University Press, 1959.

Davey, Andrew, 'Christ in the City: The Density of Presence'. In Andrew Davey, ed. *Crossover City: Resources for Urban Mission and Transformation*. London: Mowbray, 2010.

Davies, Madelaine. 'Clergy flock to fill posts in "wealthy" south-east', *Church Times*, 7th February 2014 http://www.churchtimes.co.uk/articles/2014/7-february/news/uk/clergy-flock-to-fill-posts-in-wealthy-south-east

Dixon, Marcia. 'Guns and the Cross'. *The Tablet*. 11th January 2003.

Donovan, Vincent. *Christianity Rediscovered*. 3rd edn. London: SCM, 2001.

Dorton, Andy, 'On the Estate'. In Michael Eastman and Steve Latham, eds. *Urban Church: A Practitioner's Resource Book*. London: SPCK, 2004.

Duckworth, Jenny and Justin. *Against the Tide, Towards the Kingdom*. Eugene, OR: New Monastic Library, Cascade Books, 2011.

Duncan, Malcolm. *Kingdom Come: The Local Church as a Catalyst for Social Change*. Oxford: Monarch, 2007.

Evangelical Alliance. *21st Century Evangelicals: Good News for the poor?* London: Evangelical Alliance, 2015.

Ferdinando, Keith. 'Mission: A Problem of Definition'. *Themelios* 33, no. 1, 2008: 46–59.

Flannagan, Andy. *Music and Politics*. Interview. http://www.surefish.co.uk/culture/music/2012/010612-andy-flannagan-interview.html

Fogg, Ally. 'Gunchester no more?' *The Guardian*, 3rd February 2009. http://www.guardian.co.uk/commentisfree/2009/feb/03/gun-crime-manchester-communities-police

Foster, Catherine, Crystal, and Justin Louie. *Grassroots Action and Learning for Social Change: Evaluating Community Organising*. Washington: Center for Evaluation Innovation, 2010.

Friere, Paulo. *Pedagogy of the Oppressed*. London: Penguin, 1996.

Fromont, Paul. 'Rev. W. H. Vanstone in the Suburbs'. *Prodigal Kiwi(s) Blog*, 26th November 2005. http://prodigal.typepad.com/prodigal_kiwi/2005/11/rev_w_h_vanston.html

Frost, Michael, and Alan Hirsch. *The Shaping of Things to Come*. Peabody, MA: Hendrikson, 2003.

Fryer, P. *Staying Power: The History of Black People in Britain*. London: Pluto Press, 1984.

Fung, Raymond. *The Isaiah Vision: An Ecumenical Strategy for Congregational Evangelism*. Geneva: WCC Publications, 1992.

Gamble, Robin. *The Irrelevant Church*. Tunbridge Wells: Monarch, 1991.

Gibbs, Eddie, and Ryan K. Bolger. *Emerging Churches: Creating Christian Community in Postmodern Cultures*. London: SPCK, 2006.

Gittins, Anthony J. *Called to Be Sent: Co-missioned as Disciples Today*. Liguori, Missouri: Ligouri, 2008.

Gooder, Martin, L. *The Brunswick Papers*. Manchester: self-published, 1988.

Granberg-Michaelson, Wesley. 'Covenant and Creation'. In Charles Birch, William Eaken and Jay B. McDaniel eds. *Liberating Life: Contemporary Approaches in Ecological Theology*. Maryknoll, NY: Orbis, 1990.

Green, Laurie. 'I Can't Go *There*!' In Andrew Davey ed. *Crossover City: Resources for Urban Mission and Transformation*. London: Mowbray, 2010.

Greene, Mark. *Fruitfulness on the Frontline: Making a difference where you are*. Nottingham: Inter-Varsity Press, 2014.

— — —. *Imagine: How We Can Reach the UK*. London: LICC, 2003.

Gutiérrez, Gustavo. *On Job: God-talk and the Suffering of the Innocent*. Maryknoll, NY: Orbis, 1987.

―――. *The God of Life*. London: SCM, 1991.

―――. *The Power of the Poor in History*. Maryknoll, NY: Orbis, 1983.

Hasler, Joe. *Crying out for a Polycentric Church: Christ centred and culturally focused congregations*. Maidstone: Church in Society, 2006.

Hirst, Michael. 'Location, Location, Location.' *Methodist Recorder*, 10th May 2012: 8.

Hobson, Peter. 'A Festival for Brunswick.' *Mainstream* 14, September 1983: 11–14.
http://www.biblicalstudies.org.uk/pdf/mainstream/14.pdf

Hoek, Marijke. 'Yeasting the Public Debate with Good News'. In Marijke Hoek, Jonathan Ingleby, Andy Kingston-Smith, Carol Kingston-Smith eds. *Carnival Kingdom: Biblical Justice for Global Communities*. Gloucester: Wide Margin, 2013.

Hooker, Morna D. *The Message of Mark*. London: Epworth, 1983.

Hylton, Stuart. *A History of Manchester*. Chichester: Phillimore, 2003.

Isaac, Les, and Rosalind Davies. *Street Pastors*. Eastbourne: David C. Cook, 2009.

Joslin, Roy. *Urban Harvest: Biblical Perspectives on Christian mission in the inner cities*. Welwyn: Evangelical Press, 1982.

Kaczor, Christopher. 'Seven Principles of Catholic Social Teaching', in *Catholic Answers Magazine*, Vol. 18, no. 4, April 2007.

Keeble, Paul. *A Survey of Spring Harvest Programme Seminar Information, 1996-2000*. Manchester: Urban Presence, 2001.

– – –. *Carisma: The First Ten Years*. Manchester: Carisma, October 2012.
http://www.urbanpresence.org.uk/Carisma10.pdf

– – –. 'Gang Violence'. In Michael Eastman and Steve Latham eds. *Urban Church: A Practitioner's Resource Book*. London: SPCK, 2004.

– – –. 'Mission With'. Paper presented at the Urban Theology Collective, Hawarden, North Wales, December 2007.

Kidd, Alan. *Manchester*. 4th edn. Lancaster: Carnegie, 2006.

Kohn, Tamara. 'Becoming an Islander through Action in the Scottish Hebrides'. *The Journal of the Royal Anthropological Institute* 8, no. 1, 2002: 143-158.

Kraybill, Donald B. *The Upside-Down Kingdom*. 2nd edn. Scottdale, PA: Herald, 1990.

Kreider, Alan, and Eleanor Kreider. *Becoming a Peace Church*. London: HHSC Christian Press, 2000.

LaFramboise, Teresa, Hardin L. Coleman, and Jennifer Gerton. 'Psychological Impact of Biculturalism: Evidence and Theory'. *Psychological Bulletin* 114, no. 3, 1993: 395–412.

Lane, William L. *The Gospel of Mark*. Grand Rapids, MI: Eerdmans, 1974.

Leech, Kenneth. *Doing Theology in Altab Ali Park*. London: Darton, Longman & Todd, 2006.

― ― ―. *4 Youth on the Drift* (2010) http://www.drugtext.org /pdf/Keep-The-Faith-Baby/4-youth-on-the-drift.pdf

Lingenfelter, Sherwood G., and Marvin K. Mayers. *Ministering Cross-Culturally*. Grand Rapids, MI: Baker Academic, 2003.

Linthicum, Robert C. *Building a People of Power: Equipping Churches to Transform Their Communities*. Washington DC: Authentic, 2005.

― ― ―. *Empowering the Poor: Community Organising Among the City's 'Rag, Tag and Bobtail'*. Monrovia, California: Marc, 1991.

Lovell, George. *The Church and Community Development: An Introduction*. London: Avec, 1972.

Lupton, Robert. 'Evangelism is More Than Words'. *Urban Perspectives*. Atlanta: FCS Urban Ministries, July 2012. http://fcsministries.org/blog/evangelism-is-more-than-words/

Manchester City Council. *Ardwick Local Plan*, 2008

― ― ―. *Ardwick Ward Profile 2011/2*. 2011.

Manchester Partnership, The. *Manchester's State of The Wards Report, 2010-11*. Manchester: Manchester City Council, July 2011.

― ― ―. *State of the City Report 2010/2011*. Manchester: Manchester City Council, July 2012.

McCulloch, Nigel. 'The Quiet Ministry of Support Carries On.' *Church Times*, 20th June 2008.
http://www.churchtimes.co.uk/articles/2008/20-june/comment/the-quiet-ministry-of-support-carries-on

McFee, Malcolm. 'The 150% Man: A Product of Blackfeet Acculturation'. *American Anthropologist* no. 70, 1968: 1096–1107.

McGavran, Donald. *The Bridges of God: A Study in the Strategy of Missions*. London: World Dominion Press, 1955.

Meier, John P. 'The Disciples of Christ: Who Were They?' *Mid-Stream* 38, no. 1–2, April 1999: 129–135.

Merton, Thomas. *Living Bread*. New York: Farrar, Straus & Cudahy, 1956.

Moltmann, Jürgen. *The Church in the Power of the Spirit: A Contribution to Messianic Ecclesiology*. London: SCM, 1977.

Morisy, Ann. *Beyond the Good Samaritan: Community Ministry and Mission*. London: Continuum, 1997.

———. *Journeying Out: A New Approach to Christian Mission*. London: Morehouse, 2004.

Moynagh, Michael. *emergingchurch.intro*. Oxford: Monarch, 2004.

Murray, Stuart. *Post-Christendom: Church and Mission in a Strange New World*. Carlisle: Paternoster, 2004.

———. *Church After Christendom*. Milton Keynes: Paternoster, 2004.

Myers, Bryant. *Walking With the Poor; Principles and Practices of Transformational Development*. Maryknoll, NY: Orbis, 2000.

Newbigin, Lesslie. *The Gospel in a Pluralist Society*. London: SPCK, 1989.

Nussbaum, Stan. *A Reader's Guide to Transforming Mission*. Maryknoll, NY: Orbis, 2005.

Packer, James I. *Concise Theology: A Guide to Historic Christian Beliefs*. Carol Stream, IL: Tyndale House Publishers, 2001.

Painter, John. *Mark's Gospel*. London: Routledge, 1997.

Peterson, Eugene. *The Message: The Bible in Contemporary Language*. Colorado Springs, CO: NavPress, 2004.

Pitts, John. *Reluctant Gangsters: The changing face of youth crime*. Cullompton, Devon: Willan, 2008.

Pridmore, John. *The Inner-City of God: The Diary of an East End Parson*. London: Canterbury Press, 2008.

Purnell, Derek. 'Faith Sharing'. In Michael Eastman and Steve Latham, eds. *Urban Church: A Practitioner's Resource Book*. London: SPCK, 2004.

— — —. 'Urban Presence'. In John Vincent, ed. *Faithfulness in the City*. Hawarden: Monad, 2003.

— — —. *'Speaking the Unspeakable: Who Cares About the Working Classes*. Manchester: Urban Presence, 2013.

Rohr, Richard, and Ebert Andeas. *The Enneagram: A Christian Perspective*. Campbell, CA: Crossroads, 2002.

Rowland, Chris. *Radical Christianity*. Oxford: Polity, 1988.

Alan Roxburgh. 'Reclaiming the Commons: What it is and why it is important'. *Journal of Missional Practice*, Spring 2016. http://journalofmissionalpractice.com/reclaiming-the-commons

Ruddick (née Thompson), Anna E. 'Holy Sofas: Transformational Encounters between Evangelical Christians and Post-Christendom Urban Communities'. *Practical Theology* 5, no. 1, 2012: 47–64.

Schaeffer, Francis. *Plan for Action: An Action Alternative Handbook for 'Whatever Happened to the Human Race?'*. Old Tappan, NJ: Flemming H. Revell, 1980.

Schaller, Lyle E. *Community Organisation: Conflict and Reconciliation*. Nashville: Abingdon, 1966.

Sheppard, David. *Built as a City*. London: Hodder & Stoughton, 1974.

Shropshire S. & M. McFarquhar. *Developing Multi Agency Strategies to Address the Street Gang Culture and Reduce Gun Violence Amongst Young People*. Manchester: Steve Shropshire & Michael McFarquhar Consultancy Group. September 2002.

Sine, Christine. 'Living Into God's Shalom World'. *Bible in TransMission*. Swindon: Bible Society. Spring 2008: 1–3.

Sine, Tom. 'Cultural Values'. Video, August 2010. http://www.youtube.com/watch?v=CX3HWCpt51Q

———. 'Making It Real'. *Sojourners Magazine*, January 2008. http://sojo.net/magazine/2008/01/making-it-real

———. *The New Conspirators: Creating the Future One Mustard Seed at a Time*. Bletchley: Paternoster, 2008.

———. 'The Wrong Dream'. *Tear Times*, 1996.

Smith, Austin. *Passion for the Inner City*. London: Sheed & Ward, 1983.

Smith, M. K. 'What is Praxis?' in *the encyclopaedia of informal education*. http://www.infed.org/biblio/b-praxis.htm

Sparks, Paul, Tim Soerens, Dwight J. Friesen, *The New Parish: How Neighbourhood Churches are Transforming Mission, Discipleship and Community*. Downer's Grove, Il.: InterVarsity Press, 2014.

Steuer, Nicola, and Nic Marks. *Local Wellbeing – Can We Measure it?* London: The Young Foundation, 2008.

Stott, John. *Christian Mission in the Modern World*. London: Falcon, 1975.

Strange, D. 'Co-belligerence and Common Grace: Can the Enemy of My Enemy Be My Friend?' *Cambridge Papers* 14, no. 3, 2005.

Taylor, Dr, and Mrs Howard. *Hudson Taylor's Spiritual Secret*. Chicago: Moody, 1932.

Theos. *The Whole Church, for the Whole Nation, for the Whole Year: An Evaluation of HOPE08*. London: Theos, 2009. http://www.hopetogether.org.uk/Publisher/File.aspx?ID=35144

Tillich, Paul. *Theology of Culture*. Oxford: University Press, 1959.

Tu, Janet I. 'Christian Communities Try "Whole-life Faith"'. *The Seattle Times*. 29th April 2006. http://community.seattletimes.nwsource.com/archive/?date=20060429&slug=church29m

Vincent, John. 'Basics of Radical Methodism'. In Joerg Rieger and John Vincent. *Methodist and Radical: Rejuvenating a Tradition*. Nashville: Kingswood, 2004.

— — —. *Hope from the City*. Peterborough: Epworth, 2000.

– – –. *Into the City*. London: Epworth, 1982.

– – –. 'Losing Life, Gaining Life'. In John Vincent, ed. *Mark Gospel of Action: Personal and Community Responses*. London: SPCK, 2006.

– – –. *Radical Jesus: The Way of Jesus Then and Now*. 2nd edn. Sheffield: Ashram Press, 2006.

Walker, Sara Jane. *Walking the Children to School: A Neighbourhood Story*, Journal of Missional Practice, Spring 2016. http://journalofmissionalpractice.com/author/sara-jane-walker

Walsh, Peter. *Gang War: The Inside Story of the Manchester Gangs*. Reading: Milo, 2003.

Wells, Samuel, *The Nazareth Manifesto*. Durham, NC: Duke University, 2008, https://web.duke.edu/kenanethics/Nazar ethManifesto_SamWells.pdf

– – –. *A Nazareth Manifesto: Being With God*. John Wiley & Sons, Chichester, 2015.

Williams, Eleanor. 'Urban Fresh Expressions'. Fresh Expressions. http://www.freshexpressions.org.uk/guide /examples/urban

Wilson, Matt. *Concrete Faith: The Inside Story of the Eden Network*. Manchester: Message Trust, 2012.

– – –. *Eden: Called to the Streets*. London: Kingsway, 2005.

Wood, Steve. 'When The Going Gets Tough'. *New Christian Herald*, 20 July 1996.

Wright, N. T. 'N. T. Wright on Mission – Snippets'. http://www.hopetogether.org.uk/Articles/284478/HOPE/ About_HOPE/Theology/N_T_Wright.aspx

———. *Surprised by Hope*. London: SPCK, 2007.

Yancey, Philip, *Vanishing Grace: Whatever Happened to the Good News?* London: Hodder & Stoughton, 2015.